# '30 YEAR'

The ......... of

## KEVIN 'BULLDOG' BENNETT

with Richy Horsley

www.warcrypress.co.uk
Copyright Richy Horsley ©

ISBN: 978-1-912543-09-0

30 YEARS A FIGHTER ISBN: 978-1-912543-09-0 All rights reserved. No part of this publication may be reproduced or transmitted in any form or by any means, including photocopying and recording, without the written permission of the copyright holder, application for which should be addressed to the publisher via the dealing agent at: warcrypress@roobix.co.uk, such written permission must also be obtained before any part of this publication is stored in a retrieval system of any nature. This book is sold subject to the Standard Terms and Conditions of Sale of New Books and may not be re-sold in the UK below the net price fixed by the Publisher / Agent.

30 YEARS A FIGHTER Produced by www.wacrypress.co.uk (part of Roobix Ltd: 7491233) on behalf of Richy Horsley, Hartlepool. Copyright © Richy Horsley 2018. Richy Horsley has asserted his right as the author of this work in accordance with the Copyright, Designs and Patents Act 1988.

Cover Photos by Dean Kitching

Printed and bound in Great Britain by The PMM Group

Find out more at: facebook.com/30yearsafighter/

**AMATEUR BOXING CHAMPION**

\* \* \* \*

**PROFESSIONAL BOXING CHAMPION**

\* \* \* \*

**BARE KNUCKLE BOXING CHAMPION**

## KEVIN 'BULLDOG' BENNETT

with Richy Horsley

**Dedication**

For my Children; Keeley, Jake, Zack and Molly

BOXING IS A SPORT, AN HORRIFIC SPORT
THE FIGHT FOR SURVIVAL IS THE FIGHT

- Rocky Graziano

# Acknowledgements

Many thanks to the following journalists: Roy Kelly, Ken Morton, Paul Fraser, Daniel Herbert, Bob Downing, Tony Drain, David Prior, Chris Kempson, John Jarrett, Richard Jacques, Tony Connolly and Gareth Jones. I salute you all.

Thank you to the writers of some cuttings that have no author's name.

Thanks also to Hartlepool Mail, Boxing News, Amateur Boxing Scene and Hartlepool Life.

My gratitude also goes to Andrew Close, Paddy Weldrake, Steven Smith and Luke Cope.

Front / back cover photos by Dean Kitching

# CONTENTS

INTRODUCTION                                    1

## PART ONE - AMATEUR BOXING CHAMPION

    LONG ROAD TO GLORY                 7

    CAMOUFLAGE CAPERS                  18

    ENGLAND'S NUMBER ONE               28

    NEW HORIZONS                       38

## PART TWO - PROFESSIONAL BOXING CHAMPION

    PROFESSIONAL BOXER                 52

    THE SKY IS THE LIMIT               61

    AT THE CROSSROADS                  79

    FULFILLING A DREAM                 79

    DEFENDING CHAMPION                 89

    PROFESSIONAL BOXING RECORD         98

**PART THREE - BARE KNUCKLE BOXING CHAMPION**

    BARE KNUCKLE BOXER                101

    WORLD TITLE                             108

    GOING OUT AT THE TOP           118

    BARE KNUCKLE BOXING RECORD   128

TRIBUTES AND MEMORIES                129

PHOTOGRAPHS                                178

# INTRODUCTION

I have known Kevin 'Bulldog' Bennett for the last twenty years and in that time we have been through more than other people go through in a couple of lifetimes.

I first met him when he came to Hartlepool with his pal Billy Bessey, to box for our club the Hartlepool Boys Welfare, after they both came out of the Army. He had bleached blond hair that was growing out and looked more like he was in a boy band than a fighter, but looks can be deceiving and they certainly were in Kevin's case.

As time went on and I got to know him more, I was impressed with his good manners and morals; they go a long way in my book. He can hold a good conversation about almost any topic, how many fighters do you know who has been in the game as long as him can do that!

He is a very humble and modest man and if you had just met him for the first time and didn't know anything about him, you wouldn't know that he had been a boxer for all those years because boxing would be his last topic of conversation.

He grew up in Oldbury in the West Midlands and was the middle child of five, three girls and two boys. His dad Patrick and his mum Trish instilled good values in him, and that you only get out of life what you put into it.

Kev's education was in the University of Life and he has a Master's Degree. Not many people call him Kev he is usually called Benny so that's the name we'll stick to. I can talk to him and ask his advice about anything because I know I would get an honest and intelligent answer.

I have seen him fight up and down the country and he has been the victim of some appallingly bad decisions. Although he would be gutted that he'd been blatantly robbed, he just took it on the chin like a man.

I have been in his corner many times, ABA final, pro-debut, first loss as a pro live on Sky and the bare knuckle adventure which included two world titles, to name a few. We've been through lots of highs and lows and along the way we've had some hysterically funny times.

Benny is unique as he was an amateur boxing champion, professional boxing champion and world bare knuckle boxing champion. How many people do you know have achieved that accolade?

Nobody, only Kevin Bennett, he is the first one.

He served Queen and country for over six years as a member of the Royal Logistics Corps and also fought many times for his country as an England International. I think his sporting achievements should be recognised and fingers crossed, one day he might receive an honour. Hopefully this book is the first step to that honour.

(In January 2018 he was invited to the Mayor of Hartlepool's chamber to receive an award for 'Outstanding Achievement in Sport' for his service and accomplishments in the fight game).

He had his first fight in the ring at age 11 and his last one age 41, that is three decades of trading blows, hence the book title 30 years a fighter. In reality though, Benny has been a fighter since he took his first breath in the city hospital in Birmingham back in August 1975.

I'll let his mum Trish tell you the story:

"When he was first born he wasn't very well and was in hospital on and off for the first six months. He had a lot of breathing trouble and Bronchitis and also had a touch of Bronchial Pneumonia and was on oxygen. It was very worrying but thankfully he pulled through and got better and started to thrive like any normal child."

You see Benny was a fighter as soon as he took his first breath, he had no choice, he had to fight or he wouldn't have lived. The fighting spirit was within him. He was a born fighter and on his first official trip to the scales he weighed in at six pound five ounces.

Here are some more stories from his mum Trish:

"When he was three he attempted to take his bike upstairs, there was an almighty clatter and when I ran to see what it was I realised he'd took a tumble down the stairs with his bike and broke his nose. His white t-shirt was red with blood and I was in a panic. I took him to the hospital and was hoping they didn't think I did it. The doctor was fine and said they can tell when it's an accident. Phew! What a relief.

When he was about seven years old he didn't like getting a bath and it was a nightmare trying to get him in it. I remember once when he wouldn't get in and we were arguing over it, I picked him up and dumped him in with all his clothes on and said 'now have a bath' and he just sat there with his arms folded ever so stubborn.

When he was nine he told me he wanted to be a boxer and I said to him that if he wanted to do boxing he would have to go ballet dancing as well! I was hoping it would put him off but he said he would go ballet dancing if it meant he can go boxing, so I thought 'right I'll let him go boxing but as soon as he gets punched in the face he probably won't want to go again' but it didn't put him off and he kept going.

There was a big gypsy site not far from us and he would go down there and fight the gypsy kids. Nothing ever fazed him.

He came home once with his head pouring with blood. A big kid at the bottom of the road had hit him over the head with a golf club. I went down to the house and barged my way in and pushed the mother on her backside and told the father if I got hold of the golf club I'd stick it where the sun doesn't shine. It's a good job Kevin's dad was at work or he would have gone down and decked the father.

One time when he came home on leave and we were out, his younger sister Kelly had the house full of teenagers and when they saw Kevin they scattered in all directions and the house soon cleared. Kevin hid behind a wall and when a couple of them came running past, he jumped out and got hold of them and banged their heads together and told them to keep out. The funny thing is Kelly ended up marrying one of the lads who got his head banged and we've had a laugh about it a few times."

Benny is many things, father, husband, family man, brother, uncle, role model, champ, loyal friend, joker, pugilist, too many to mention. He was best man at my wedding to Wendy and it is a pleasure and an honour to call him my friend.

I will remind you that this isn't about his private life, just his memories of the fight game, although you will read about some funny things.

I could go on and on but I won't, I'll pass you over to the man himself and let him take you through his fighting memoirs, in his own words.


Thank You

*Richy Horsley*

# PART ONE

# AMATEUR BOXING CHAMPION

# ROUND 1

# LONG ROAD TO GLORY

I can't remember much about my very early years, hardly anything, but I can remember when I first started boxing. I was nine years old and attending Causeway Green primary school in Oldbury; when a friend called Barry asked me and a couple of other lads if we fancied going to the boxing gym so we said yes why not. I remember it was winter and he already had bandages on his hands when he came to my house. My friends and I went along thinking it would be a laugh but I really enjoyed it. Barry had been going regularly and had all the gear but we just had our basic stuff and not any of the fancy boxing attire like him. After a couple of months the lads stopped going and then even Barry packed it in but I took to it and started going on my own. I was quite a cocky kid, a bit loud and always the joker so I think it suited my personality a little bit. It was a three mile walk to the gym from our house (a good hike for a little nipper like me) so I was doing six miles every time I went and I walked whatever the weather. I recall it was 25 pence a session and the coaches were Reg Snooks and Arthur Clayton. Arthur had fought the great Randolph Turpin back in the day and was only at the club another few years and retired, he'd done his bit. Dennis Jackson took his place.

My parents bought me a pair of boxing boots and I was buzzing, I would have slept in them if I could. I flashed them off at a skills day when everyone was assessed to see how well they were doing and I got a Gold medal. It was nice to hear people comment on how much I'd improved. I was still only 10 and wasn't allowed to have an actual bout until I was 11. I think that is still the rule to this day.

Some night's after training I would stop back and watch the senior boxers train and spar. They were coached by a man named Reg Steel and I'd watch like a hawk and absorb as much as I could and try the different moves out the next time I was in the gym.

While I was training and dreaming of my first real boxing fight I had a few bare knuckle fights with the Gypsy lads. There was a patch of wasteland about a mile from our house called the billings or the billy-bongs or something like that where people from our area used to play on their bikes.

One day a load of Gypsy trailers pulled on and stayed there for about eight months or so. Some of the Gypsy kids came to our school and the lads liked to fight. Most of the lads at school were intimidated by them but they always found me accommodating because I liked to fight too. After having a couple of fights with them, I got to know the lads a little and sometimes I'd go to their site with them and there was always someone wanting to put their fists up. Will you fight this one or that one or 'will you fight him over there', it was just the way they were. I had a few fights on the Gypsy camp and never lost any.

I was 11in August 1986 and I got my medical to say I was fit to box and around late September or early October, I was matched up and ready for my first fight. I was pretty excited and couldn't wait for fight night. During the passing of time I've forgot my first opponent's name but it was at the Kingfisher Country Club and I won a unanimous decision. I was on top of the world and couldn't wait to tell my parents and siblings and all my friends at school. Benny the boxer was on his way.

After the exhilaration of my first win came the disappointment of my first loss to the aptly named Mark Virgin. My coach, myself and many others in the audience thought I won but I lost on a majority. I won my next three and fought him again. This time I broke my thumb in the first round and lost on another majority. He disappeared off the circuit after that and I never heard of him boxing on any shows. He may have had one or two seasons and packed it in but I couldn't break my duck against mister virgin.

The next season I had 12 fights and 12 wins and was progressing nicely. I entered the national schoolboy championships and in the regional semi-final I beat a lad called Philip Jones and then became regional champ when I beat someone called T. Brown. I reached the national quarter-finals losing a very close majority decision to Jason Cook from Wales, who went on to win European and IBO World title's as a pro.

I started training with the senior team when I was 14 and was racking up win after win but was unlucky again in the championships when I lost out to a very talented southpaw called Gareth Lawrence.

I've lost count of the times I've been in the gym training and the coach comes in and says:

"Have you got your boots and gum-shield because you are boxing tonight" and off you went it was as simple as that. You'd be on your way to a boxing show and fighting.

It was at one of these shows that I saw a boxer with a broken nose for the first time and I thought he really looked the part, just how I imagined a boxer to look and mentioned it to my coach; who gave me some words of advice that I've never forgot when he said:

"Don't worry about him son, worry about the pretty boy in the corner who done it to him."

In the NABC championships the next year I beat all my opponents inside the distance until the semi-final and I was getting a little ink in my local rag. Unfortunately the reporter's name isn't on it so I don't know who wrote it but thank you whoever you are.

**Another Cowdell in the making?**

Warley ABC; believe they have discovered another Pat Cowdell in 16-year-old featherweight Kevin Bennett, who took only 60 seconds to dispose of his opponent in the NABC Midland championships.

His first round knock-out makes him favourite to go a step further when he meets Western Counties champion Courtney Thomas at Bristol on April11 with a place in the quarter-finals to be held at Wolverhampton two weeks later as the prize.

Bennett, fast and clever and clearly carrying a powerful punch in Cowdell style, has made great strides since he was beaten in the schools quarter-finals last year.

Another little write up (no author's name) reads:

Warley featherweight Kevin Bennett is taking the quick route to the NABC championships. He took less than a round to dispose of his opponent in the regional final at Bristol and will go into the national semi-finals in Wolverhampton next week as a strong favourite to reach the final.

Bennett hailed as another Pat Cowdell by his coach Denis Jackson, floored the Western Counties champion, Courtney Thomas twice before the referee stepped in to stop the contest. It lasted just 40 seconds and the Warley ABC coach said today: "Kevin is the brightest young prospect we have seen for years. He is quick, clever and packs a powerful punch. I'm confident he will go all the way."

## Bennett powers on

"Warley ABCs Kevin Bennett is through to the NABC finals following another impressive performance in the semi-finals at Wolverhampton on Saturday.

The 16-year-old gained a unanimous points decision over Aaron Williamson of Leeds and now fights in the finals at Bristol on May 8.

Southpaw Williamson had won his three previous contests by knock-out but Bennett hurt him in the opening round and went on to dictate tactics and outbox his rugged opponent."

May 8 I fought in the Class B, NABC final, it was my 68$^{th}$ amateur fight. I fought Steven Whyte from Medway who had won 35 out of his 40 fights and not only was he a dangerous puncher, he was also a very skilled boxer and I missed out on a close decision. I drowned my sorrows afterwards and got drunk for the first time, it was on the coach on the way home and there were loads of us as I always had a good following and I spewed all over my Dad's shoes! You can imagine he was over the moon about that.

All the national champions and runners up were invited to a training weekend at Keele University in East Anglia. You trained and sparred with all the best lads from all over the country. Imagine the testosterone that was flying around as everyone was trying to prove themselves. Lads strutting around with chests out thinking they were cock of the walk. I sparred with Tony Oakey and closed his eye. He said something sarcastic to me and I offered him outside but he didn't fancy it.

Years later me and a pal were giving him a lift to England training camp and he said to me:

"I remember you from Keele University when you shut my eye and offered me out,"

I said "My god was that you!"

"Yes" he answered and we had a good laugh about it.

Tony became British, Commonwealth and WBU Light-Heavyweight champion as a pro.

Another good lad who I fought on the circuit was Lee Woodley who would later turn pro under the name Young Mutley and win the British title. I fought him twice and beat him both times.

There were so many clubs around at that time and they all seemed to have two or three lads at my weight, I was practically fighting every other week and I had that many fights it's hard to remember a lot of them. There was a fight I had with a lad from Aston called Johnny Fellows that made the local paper and the journalist who wrote it was called Bob Downing.

**Classy contest**

"Kevin Bennett and Johnny Fellows had the crowd on their feet at the IMI Social Club in Aston last Thursday. Neither of them wasted a second in piling up points with jabs, crosses and combinations. It was six minutes of non-stop explosive action and Bennett just shaded it on the judge's scorecards. Two judges scored it 59-58 for Bennett and the third judge scored it the same way for Fellows. Johnny Fellows has shown tremendous improvement over the last 12 months while Kevin Bennett has long been a star in the making from Warley."

After leaving school I became an apprentice welder. I was doing well standing on my own two feet, making my own money and feeling all grown up, then after so many months the firm laid quite a few people off and I was one of them. I was sat about twiddling my thumbs and I needed to be busy, I wasn't one to sit around on the bones of my arse with no money, I was a go getter. I didn't fancy going on a YTS as my dad said it was slave labour, so one day I went down to the Army careers office and ended up joining the Royal Logistics Corps.

My parents threw me a leaving party and all my pals turned up, what a great night we had. When it was time to say goodbye at the train station my mam broke her heart. It was my first time away from home but you know what. I loved it. They say one man's medicine is another man's poison and I saw that at first hand. Some of the new recruits were crying all the time wanting to go home, someone actually went AWOL after only two days but I took to it like a duck to water.

They would pick different people to be in charge of the squadron for the day and you would march them about etc and this particular day it was my turn. We had only been there around a month, so the squadrons who had been there longer were in charge of us and that was how they brought you through. The lad in charge of a squadron who had been there about six months was a 6ft 2in Light-Heavyweight boxer known as China because he had slanty eyes.

I was out at the front of the squad and he came over shouting at me wanting to know what I was doing.

"I am the duty NCO today Sergeant" I said. He was a Junior Sergeant but we still had to call him Sergeant.

"Well nobody has told me so get in line" he screamed.

"I'm only doing as I'm told and who the fuck do you think you are talking to?"

"Who do you think you are" he said "You think you are hard, I'll meet you in the Naafi tonight and we'll sort it"

"No problem. I'll fight you no bother" came my response.

I grew up in a working class area and had been fighting all my life so I didn't give a second thought to an arsehole like him.

Anyway we weren't allowed in the Naafi that night and I was in my room quietly polishing my boots when he came storming into the room full of hell with two of his mates.

"Let's have it then!" he said as he stood over me.

I jumped up and grabbed him and threw him down and started smashing punches into his head and one of his pals pulled me off.

"You might be hard but I'll cut your throat" were his parting words. I never had any more trouble from him and it done my reputation no harm at all.

I flew through basic training and when we done the inter-squadron boxing some of the sergeants knew I was a boxer so they had bets on me and I won both my fights inside 30 seconds.

I got picked to box in the Junior Army championships down in Wiltshire. All the lads went on home leave that weekend but I went down the country to fight. I won both my fights in the first round and became Junior Army champion.

I boxed for the 7 Transport Regiment against 2$^{nd}$ Battalion Royal Anglican in the Inter-Unit championships. In the forces magazine (no author's name) it said: "The light-welter contest between Pte Bennett and Pte Allen started with a fiery attack by both fighters. Bennett, the smaller of the two, hit hard but Allen was stronger in body and it was clear it was going to be a hard fight. A penalty in the second round for punching below the belt cost Bennett dearly but it did not stop an accurate display of hard punches from finding their target, and Bennett emerged the winner."

I also had aspirations of going in the SAS and the RCM of the regiment had a couple of his friends in the SAS who would come and visit him. The next time they came to visit, he sent for me –nobody else just me- to go and meet them.

There would be about 400 soldiers on the square in their squadrons and the RCM would have everyone stood to attention while he addressed everybody and he'd shout:

"Private Bennett where are you?"

I would shout my name and he would come to where I was and shout for everyone to hear:

"Are you still the hardest in the regiment Bennett?"

"Sir" meaning yes sir,

"Does anyone think they can take Bennett" he would holler and no one would say anything.

"Do you think you could take me Bennett?"

"No Sir,"

"I know that Bennett" he'd say with half a smile.

When I was in basic training I participated in numerous sporting events and activities like swimming, running, rugby, shooting, boxing, etc. I always loved sports so you could say I was a bit of an all-rounder. I played rugby for the regiment team and also played for a civvy team called Wool Lions from Dorset. I represented the regiment in swimming and cross country running and obviously boxing. I did very well in a mini-pentathlon which included swimming, shooting and running. I won the inter-squadron champs and the junior army champs at boxing. At our passing out parade I received the best all-round sportsman award. It was a great day and my family were as proud as punch.

# ROUND 2

# CAMOUFLAGE CAPERS

Did I say I flew through basic training? Well there was a misdemeanour or two. We went on adventure training at fort something or other in a place called Tall Point. It was an escape and evasion exercise. The permanent staff came in the room with guns and made us all line up against the wall like it was a hostage situation. We were all stripped naked and searched to make sure nobody had anything on their person. Then we were given a pair of Army issue coveralls, a pair of boots with no laces, a waterproof jacket and a map. You are paired off with another lad and in teams of two you had to escape out of the fort.

There are various checkpoints on the map and when you make it to the first one, you will get information were to go next. You had to avoid capture at all times. You can imagine a load of squaddies running around at daft o'clock in the morning trying to avoid being captured.

Me and the lad I was paired with who was called Taylor, couldn't believe our luck when we spotted a milk float. It was like an oasis in the desert. We were really thirsty and hungry but soon were both disappointed when there were no strawberry yoghurts on board; but Alas, cartons of orange juice. We didn't move too far away before we started guzzling down the liquid refreshment and as we are doing this, the milk float flew round the corner and screeched to a halt. The furious milkman is screaming and shouting at us and grabs hold of Taylor and starts ragging him about all over the place. I did what anyone else would do in that situation and chinned the milkman!

I hit him with a right hand straight on the chin and he went down like a sack of spuds. When we arrived at the next checkpoint the permanent staff where asking everybody if they knew anything about an incident with a milkman, no one knew anything but there was now a police presence.

The final aim of the exercise was to get back into the fort to complete the mission, but when we got back there was a lot of police there. The milkman turned up and pointed me out straight away.

Taylor and I had to get our best clobber on, all highly polished and smart as carrots, and go to the milk man's house with cap in hand and apologize. We took him four cans of beer, bought his wife some flowers and gave him five pounds for the orange juice we'd stolen. We were told by the military we'd hear no more about it, but when we got back to our regiment we had to go in front of the Regiment Corporal Major and he charged us. Now listen to this for a charge and have you ever heard anything like it:

'Improper possession of a carton of orange juice' and 'bringing the Army's name into disrepute'

Improper possession of a carton of orange juice! I thought it was a wind up. At least he didn't press charges but what a piss take. We were both fined £100 which was a week's wage for us at the time. These exercises are supposed to be real life situations and in real life situations you do things you wouldn't normally do. What the hell did they expect us to do? Thinking back now I should have made him knock us up a fuckin' omelette!

Once during 'pay parade' everyone was lined up in alphabetical order to go in the office and receive our money. I was second or third as B for Bennett was near the front. Everyone's money was on the table in different piles with forms to sign to say you'd received it. You were allowed £20 per week for things like tooth paste, boot polish and other essentials. The rest of your money was put into the bank. At the time we were still learning drill and you had to march up to the table, halt in front of it, salute and say your name, rank and number, sign the paperwork and say "pay correct sir."

As you can imagine; with me being second or third, the table was piled high with money. I marched up to the table and misjudged the space so when I brought my knee up, I lifted the table up and all the money went everywhere!

I laughed nervously and the lieutenant shouted 'Get him away' and ordered me jailed for a few hours. Easy mistake I'm sure I wasn't the first or last.

Despite the couple of misdemeanours, I was doing lots of Army training and enjoying the whole experience but whenever our squad got beasted, I was the only one who had to do one handed press ups. I was a boxer and good at press ups so they would make it harder for me but I loved it. I did my trade training to become a driver and also done pre-commando training and passed everything with flying colours. While all this was going on and I was establishing myself with my regiment, 12 months had gone by and I hadn't boxed once because of it. Then I was sent to Germany with the 7th Regiment which was also a boxing regiment within the Royal Logistics Corps and when I arrived there I had to go and see the boxing coach and he told me to come back at ten o'clock with my gear and he'd 'have a look at me.'

When I went back I was put in the ring with a lad called Chris Stock who was the first person to beat Joe Calzaghe as an amateur. Everyone was watching and I got the better of the spar and it made a lot of people sit up and take notice. I went from strength to strength from that moment. I've never been a fan of pitter-patter sparring it's a waste of time, I like to get stuck in and have a pop.

I was straight on the regiment team and at that time we were in the final of the forces abroad competition and our opposition were the Royal Anglian Regiment. I won my fight and we won the final. I was picked to fight in a special bout against someone from the King's Regiment in a place called Sella. I won the fight and after that I got upgraded from the Regiment team to the Army team. I had another couple of wins against decent opponents and when the Army team was announced that would go forward and fight in the combined services, there was an objection at my weight from a lad called Karl Hilton. I think he was from the Kings Regiment and had been the Army representative at light-welter for the past two years and he thought he was being overlooked. Everyone called him psycho because that's how he fought and he had mad eyes. His strength and punch power was phenomenal and he was knocking people out for fun. He was a dangerous banger and his left hook had dynamite in it. A box off was arranged and we fought in the gym behind closed doors. We had three judges and a referee and it was all done properly as you would imagine with the Army.

He came at me from the first bell trying to take me out but I bobbed and weaved and hit back. The people in attendance said it was a barnstormer and by the third he had shot his bolt and was taking a lot of punishment and the ref stopped it. I went forward to the combined services as the Army rep at my weight.

I beat a Royal Marine and was presented with a cup by former World champ Terry Marsh. Then I beat someone from the RAF called Mackay and became combined services champion. Next it was Combined Services Boxing Association v London ABA with the winners going through to the ABA quarter-finals. I fought a lad who was highly regarded called Craig Stanley who was the NABC champion. I gave him a couple of standing counts and won on points. After that fight I was rated in the top ten in the country for the first time and it was a real buzz seeing my name in the boxing news amateur ratings. A paper cutting (no author's name) from then reads:

## ARMY BEAT THE PRIDE OF LONDON

"An emerging squad of Army boxers began their representative programme with an encouraging 6-4 win over a London ABA select team at Stoke-on-Trent.

New coach RSM Tom O'Connor has had 25 men in training at Aldershot and was reducing his squad to 20 by the

Christmas break. There were several encouraging performances with newcomer Pte Kevin Bennett setting the standard when he unanimously outpointed International Craig Stanley in a light-welterweight match.

Coach O'Connor was impressed by Bennett's skill, strength, timing and mobility."

Next up was the quarter-finals of the ABA championships and I beat a good lad called Jason Hall. Tony Drain of the Amateur boxing scene said:

"Bennett controlled the first round, his heavier shots, particularly his left hook, finding the target and causing Hall problems. The Londoner began to find his opponent with his long left jab in the middle session but some of his work lacked authority up until the final round. In those three minutes he upped his work rate, constantly firing home straight combinations. The judge's decision clearly revolved around the outcome of the second round, two saw it for Bennett, one for Hall, all on scores of 59-58."

In the national semi-final on 28 March 1995 at Portsmouth I fought Lance Crosby. I was given a warning in the third round for coming in with my head low. It was a 'nothing' warning but it cost me a place in the final because I lost a majority decision in a fight I thought I was very unlucky not to be given the nod.

A piece in the amateur boxing scene magazine by Tony Drain said:

"In a very tight clash at light-welter between Hull's Lance Crosby and Army's Kevin Bennett was probably decided by a last round warning against Bennett for 'low head' with the judges returning a split verdict in the Hull boxers favour. Both boxers worked from behind tight defensive stances, Crosby landed the cleaner crisper shots on my card but Bennett's hooks made it a very close call."

I came within a hairs breadth of the ABA final. I had certainly had a great season and was rated in the top four in the country at light-welterweight.

You had certain privileges in the Army team as they always look after their boxers. You didn't have to do guard duty as well as many other things and you were allowed home at weekends if you weren't boxing in any championships or tournaments.

This weekend I went up to stay at one of the lads' houses and a friend from the Parachute Regiment came and we planned on painting the town red. We were going from pub to pub and having a good night then all hell broke out in one boozer and we just stood watching this big fight take place. Then someone grabbed our Para mate and pulled his jumper over his head and started laying into him for no reason. My pal and I were laughing and the Para got his jumper back on straight and addressed the guy with "Is that the best you can do."

The bloke ignored him because he had his eyes on his next victim, me! He came towards me and as he got in range I hit him with a peach of a shot CRACK and he was out cold.

The Police turned up and we done a runner with them in hot pursuit. My other pal who wasn't involved in the fight was running at the back and because he knew the area he was shouting 'Left' so we'd turn left, 'Right' and we'd turn right. Then I heard a loud URGH and he was down with the cops on top of him but we got away and I went to the Para's house and we enjoyed the rest of the weekend drinking in his town. Our friend was kept in the cells for a couple of days but was released without charge.

We did have some fun on the boxing team; it wasn't all strict training and dieting. Another night I was the worse for wear and a fight broke out and I was scrapping. I dropped some bloke and because I was so drunk, I fell over him and ended up with a big carpet burn on my head.

When a new regiment member got invited to the Naafi for the first time he would have to go through an initiation. Boxers seemed to be exempt from this for some reason so I didn't have to do it but my first time in there I saw it happen. How it worked was somebody would get a glass and have a whip round and everyone would put money in the pot. They would then get a pint of 'top shelf' which meant every short on the top shelf shot into a pint glass. The new recruit would be stood on a stool with his trousers and underwear pulled down to his ankles and everyone would sing this certain song. After the song was sung, the recruit would have so many seconds to drink it down and what was left was poured over his head. As you can imagine as soon as the effects of the spirits hit him, he was in a heap on the floor pissed out of his mind.

I bet you are all wondering why I have never mentioned any girlfriends by now. Would you believe me if I told you that boxing was my first love. I didn't really have many love interests as I was too busy being one of the lads. My first ever girlfriend at junior school was a girl called Lucy Tinsel. My sisters used to tease me and call her tinsel off the Christmas tree. She used to live around the corner and went to my school. We were just young kids so it was never going to last long and it didn't.

A couple of girlfriends I recall from my senior school Warley High are Rachel Whyle and Elizabeth Wythes. Neither of them were what you would call long term relationships and both fizzled out before you could call them long term. I was never short of female admirers so why would I want to be in a committed relationship when I could play the field and see who I wanted to; it's a no brainer isn't it. I did go out with Rachel a few times for a couple of months at a time. She was like a boomerang she kept coming back.

My first 'serious' relationship, if that's what you want to call it, was with a girl called Jayne Jukes. I had been in the forces about a year or so when we met. She was my sister's next door neighbour and we lived together for about two years. We were together at weekends when I wasn't away boxing and kept in touch by phone during the week. One day at the shopping centre we had a massive row, it was over something stupid really, and that was it, I was done. I got my clothes and moved out. Her brother phoned me saying she was upset and crying all the time and wanted us to get back together, but I just said it was over and it was time to move on because the relationship had run its course and that was that.

One weekend on home leave I bumped into Rachel again. I hadn't seen her in years and I dropped her off at home. She said she had a boyfriend but they weren't serious and asked me to go round and see her which I did. I parked my car round the corner and went in. We had a great time getting acquainted again, then when I was having a bath the doorbell rang and she shouted 'It's him' with a bit of panic in her voice. I jumped out the bath and wrapped a towel around myself and was sat in the airing cupboard listening to them arguing and all the while thinking to myself 'Isn't this fuckin' nice.' I'm only glad he didn't come upstairs and find my hiding place because it would have been embarrassing for everyone.

Other times when I was on home leave and my dad needed someone to help out on the doors I'd find myself working as a bouncer at Buzby's in West Bromwich. My dad ran a few doors and sometimes he'd be let down at the last minute and if I was home I'd help out. I didn't like bouncing it wasn't my cup of tea but there was no trouble when I was working which was fortunate. The only trouble I had was fighting the women off. My dad and the other doormen would get asked on a weekly basis from women 'Is Kevin working tonight', 'When is Kevin working again', 'Is he home from the Army this week', you would think I was a young hunk of burning love. I don't know where they got that impression from!

# ROUND 3

# ENGLAND'S NUMBER ONE

When you were on the Army boxing team, you were weighed every single day and your weight was logged to see that you didn't stray too far away from your fighting weight. I've seen lads boiling themselves down trying to make weight especially for the championships.

Training three times a day as well as going running at night in all their sweat gear. Some didn't dare brush their teeth because they wouldn't be able to drag themselves off the tap. It's a torturous thing to do. Everyone had their own method, some would sit in baths of boiling water and sweat that way while others would suck on a lemon and dry out through the night. I remember skipping in the sauna trying to make lightweight for the championships.

When I boxed for England out in Estonia in the Multi-Nations, I was fighting a Russian at lightweight and I was killing myself to make the weight. It was the middle of winter and bitter cold so I went out running with all my sweat gear on and when I got back 30 minutes later I didn't have a bead of sweat on me. I was skipping until midnight the night before the fight and then dried out during the night. The next morning I was still a little over and had to go in the sauna. That is the one thing about boxing that I'll never miss. I always thought it was the worst part.

I did turn up overweight for England training once and when I got on the scales I weighed 71kgs! The coaches were fuming with me being over a stone overweight and put me in to spar with Alan Page and the Middleweight champion John Pearce.

Most England times were good times when not trying to make weight. When you were training with the national team at Crystal Palace they liked you to stay in, it was training all the way and they were very strict like that. I usually stuck to the rules. I did say usually.

I'm not naming names but myself and a couple of the lads went out for a drink and all three of us pulled and we all went back to one of the lasses flats. The next morning we were heading back to camp in a taxi as the morning run was almost upon us, when one of the lads realises he has left his wallet. None of us could remember any of their names! The taxi turned around and headed back to where it picked us up from. The flat was on the second or third floor and my mate is outside shouting

"Oi I've left my wallet"

Well as luck would have it his wallet comes flying out the window and we made haste to get back to camp for the morning run.

On a trip to Denmark with the national team we were out socialising in a nightclub celebrating our win and one of the boxer's fathers started fighting. I got involved and ended up chinning someone and the police came in and arrested me. There I was sat handcuffed in the back of a police car thinking my England career was over, when one of the boxers comes out of the club with two women. He comes over and speaks to the cops and tells them I'm an England boxer over here on boxing duty for my country etc and they tell him if he takes me straight back to the hotel they will let me go without any charges. So in the space of a few minutes I went from being handcuffed in the back of a police car and thinking my England career was down the toilet, to being released with no charges and on my way back to the hotel with two women. What a result.

This season just before the ABA championships I fought Carl Wall who was one of the best amateurs in the country. It was a very competitive fight and I beat him by decision and felt confident that this year was going to be my year.

I went in the ABAs at lightweight and my Army team mate Vinny Powell went in at light-welter. Vinny was a cracking fighter who was a Welsh International. Each year we would swap weights so next year he would be in at lightweight and I'd be at the heavier light-welterweight. We did this mainly for the combined services to mess the Navy and Air Force about so they didn't know who was going in at what weight.

I raced through the combined services and was crowned champion again with a first round knock-out against an RAF guy but this time at the lower weight. Then I was in the national quarter-finals at the York Hall in Bethnal Green against the hometown boy Kelvin Wing. David Prior who covered the fights for ABS magazine wrote:

"Kevin Bennett looked to be hustling Kelvin Wing out of the lightweight scene during the early part of their three rounds, forcing the Repton boxer into somewhat untidy exchanges. But with the excitement at fever pitch in the last round, Wing outpunched Bennett and landed a few jabs near the end to confirm a narrow 15-13 verdict."

I don't know what fight he was watching but Wing did not outpunch me. I lost 15-13 on the computer scoring in a fight I thought I won. Kelvin was a lovely stylist with good footwork but I feel if it was manual scoring I would have won. I don't think the computer system was a fair system.

Kelvin was profiled in the ABS magazine by Chris Kempson who wrote: "Continuing on his home turf of Bethnal Green, Kelvin was soon to face his toughest championship test so far when he came up against Kevin Bennett. Army strong man Bennett, out-hustling Kelvin over the first three minutes. Wing had to dig deep to force Bennett back in the second session and then jabbed well in the final stages of the last round to clinch a tight 15-13 verdict. It had been quite a battle."

Kelvin Wing said: "He was very strong indeed and I lost the first round. I had to fight him and overcome him, which I eventually managed to do. I prefer to box my opponents."

Everyone had their own opinion and in my opinion I won that fight. If it was on my own patch, I would have got the nod instead of him but that's just the way it goes. The hometown fighter gets the luck. Kelvin went on to be crowned ABA lightweight champ and Carl Wall who I had beaten just before the championships started, won the ABA title at light-welterweight that same year.

After the Kelvin Wing fight I got picked to fight for England in the Multi-Nations for the first time and I was training a lot at Crystal Palace with the England squad. That year they were being held in Liverpool and there were a lot of talented fighters from the USA, Canada, Russia and loads of other countries. I fought a highly skilled lad from the Ukraine and got outpointed. He was a southpaw who fenced with his lead hand. He caught me with a body shot that I can still feel now. He whipped the shot in, in bolo fashion and it landed right in my solar plexus and almost doubled me in half. I backed up to the ropes and as he came in to unload, I threw a right hand over the top that caught him flush and visibly wobbled him and the ref gave him a standing count. It was a good fight.

I was fighting all over the country on the club circuit when we got a call for two fighters that were needed for a big London show. One of the London clubs –I forget which one- were fighting a New York Police team from America and they needed a light-welter and a featherweight because they didn't have anyone good enough at those weights to fight the yanks, so Darren 'Dazzo' Williams and I got the job. I fought a Hispanic guy, I think he was called Rodriguez and I beat him in a good scrap. My pal Darren also won. Darren 'Dazzo' Williams went on to be British champ as a pro. Not long ago I was talking to an old Army boxing team member who said the talent in the Army team at that time was probably the best it has ever been. Almost everyone won British or Commonwealth titles as pros.

Out of all the people I've sparred with, Chris Bessey was the most awkward. Chris was England captain many times in an illustrious career which also seen him honoured with an MBE. A southpaw who had deceivingly long arms a bit like King Louie from the jungle book, you'd think you were well out of range and thud! He would bust your lips with his jab. When you got close to him he would tie you up. I've seen him fight world champions and make them look ordinary. He boxed the lugs off Marcus Beyer who was world champ and he also schooled Carl Froch in the ABA final. He is one of the best I've seen. No wonder he won six ABA titles and a Gold medal at the Commonwealth Games.

Irish champion and national hero Francis Barrett, who carried Ireland's flag during the opening ceremony of the '96 Olympic Games in Atlanta only a few months previous, was boxing for the Trojan club and was gearing up for a tilt at the 1997 ABA championships at Welterweight. They had a big show coming up in London and they wanted Francis as the main star attraction.

I went down and fought him and gave a lump of weight away but I wasn't bothered about that, it was just another fight to me. We were last fight of the night and the place was packed to the rafters. He was a stocky southpaw and very strong and rugged who kept coming forward and got me on the back foot; but sometimes I prefer it that way because I was a good counter puncher off the front or back foot. There were stages when I pushed him back but for most of it I boxed on the back foot because it was easier and suited the style of the fight.

Although he came forward, I found him quite easy to hit and he took a lot of shots on the way in, but he was tough and soaked it up and he was pleased to hear the bell when it finished.

It was a hell of a fight which was awarded 'fight of the night' and he won a majority decision. The hero has always got to win. His coach apologised to me about the decision but I wasn't too fussed about it. His ABA campaign went brilliant and he won the title at Welterweight.

They made a documentary about him called, Southpaw: The Francis Barrett Story. It followed him for three years up until the Olympic Games. If you get a chance to check it out it's worth watching.

I swept through the combined services again and in the ABA quarter finals I was up against a seriously talented lad called Michael Hall who was an established International and was ABA Welterweight champion two years before. Michael was very well thought of throughout the boxing circles. I immediately put the pressure on him but he was very clever on the back foot. He looked almost lazy as if he didn't want to engage but he was a very good and clever boxer. I threw a lot more punches and thought I won it clearly enough but they announced the decision as a draw so they went to a count back and he got the nod. Michael went on to fight Ricky Hatton in the final and was very unlucky to lose by one point in a fight that could have gone either way. You are talking very small margins between success and failure at that level.

The computer scoring never really suited my style. It was suited to the stand-up boxer and became more like fencing than boxing. That was one of the reasons I wanted to turn professional. I was a body puncher and always have been and they never seemed to score body punches. It really was a controversial scoring system. I was short and liked to get inside and throw body punches so it never suited my style. I'm glad it's going back to how it used to be by getting rid of the computer scoring and head guards. It's about time. Although I would like to say to any amateur that reads this is, if you are at the top level you should go for funding and stay amateur. If you are an amateur and think you have done as much as you can and want to turn pro, I'd say give it a go because you will never forgive yourself if you don't. You will need to put your heart and soul into it and don't make the mistake of cutting corners. When you walk away from the sport, do it knowing that you have given it your best shot.

It was getting harder for me to get fights because very few people wanted to fight me apart from in the championships so it was hard to do the club shows but I did manage to get a fight with a very dangerous puncher called Gary Reid. I boxed well, bobbing, slipping, hitting him with counters, keeping tucked up and won a unanimous decision.

I went back on International duty abroad again, and this time I had the honour of being captain of the England team against the Danes in Denmark. I was up against their number one man, Mehmet Erarslan. When I looked in the programme I couldn't believe the amount of titles he had already won. He was a pressure fighter and came straight at me but he seemed to be made for me and I gave him a leather shampoo for three rounds. I won the fight easily enough but he got the decision and it made headlines in the amateur section of the next issue of Boxing News: "Bennett robbed in Denmark."

A week later we flew to Dublin to fight Ireland in another International and I boxed a lad called Michael Kelly, who was very tough and came for a go, but he couldn't get through with anything and I won with plenty in hand.

On the programme they put that I was from the Army and I was hoping there was nobody in the crowd who was going to shoot me! I didn't know why I was worried because I didn't get a hostile reception. I think boxing bridges that gap. Lots of future professional stars were on the England team on that show including Carl Froch, David Haye and Audley Harrison.

I had toyed with the idea of leaving the Army the year before but had second thoughts and withdrew my notice to leave. If you wanted to leave the Army you had to give them 12 month notice so this time when I put my name down to leave I had no intentions of withdrawing it. My decision was based on a few things.(1) Partly because the money wasn't very good (2) Partly because it had gone stale and I wasn't doing anything military (3) Partly because I wanted to be a pro boxer and you can't do that if you are in the Army. They wanted me to start getting on with my career but by that point I had lost interest. I'd been wearing tracksuits most of the time and rarely done anything military apart from my basic training and didn't want to go back to that so that's when I made the decision to leave and put my notice in.

I won the combined services title for the fourth year in a row and this time I didn't have to throw a punch because no one at my weight would fight me. I thought this was going to be my year when I would win the ABA title and fight in the Commonwealth Games. I had established myself as England number one at light-welterweight and was a regular on the International circuit and it was usually the ABA champions who were selected for the Commonwealth Games.

On 5 Feb 1998 at RAF Cosford in Shropshire I was up against Nigel Wright in the quarter finals. I had already seen him box, he was a young lad, only about 18 or 19 years old and he was a southpaw with fast hands. I didn't think that much about him and to tell the truth, I thought it was going to be easy and I underestimated him.

By his own admittance he boxed scared that night but it was the fear that was the magic ingredient for him and it did the trick. I disregarded him and paid the price. I chased him for three rounds and just couldn't get my shots off. He was too sharp and covered a lot of ground and he beat me fair and square. That victory gave him the confidence to go on and win the ABA title because he must have thought if he can beat me he can beat anyone. My ABA dream went up in smoke and so did my selection for the Commonwealth Games as Nigel got selected.

All the England boxers who fought at the Commonwealths got their hair dyed blond for the games that year. Even some of us who didn't go had our hair dyed as well. The idea came from the European football championships from two years before when one of the teams did it.

Although not going to the games as the light-welterweight rep was a bitter pill to swallow, I was still an England regular and got called up for the Multi-Nations.

My first fight was against a guy from Finland and I won all three rounds pretty comfortably and won the decision. The next round I was drawn against a Ukrainian. I always got drawn against the Russians or the Ukrainians who were in the world top ten rankings. They always had shit hot teams and their boxers were second to none. This Ukrainian whose name I can't recall, was one of the best boxers I've ever seen. He was a southpaw, I hated fighting southpaws, and he had everything. As soon as I got my feet to where I wanted them, he was out of range. I certainly wasn't going to outscore him over three rounds no matter how hard I tried. The Ukrainians were on another level, you only have to look at Vasyl Lomachenko to see that.

You know when I said earlier that fear was the key ingredient for Nigel Wright when he beat me in the ABAs? Fear can be the key or the killer it depends on the individual. You can make it work for you like Nigel did or work against you. I've seen both cases. Everyone gets a few nerves but there's a difference between nerves and fear. If you let fear get the better of you, you will have no energy or strength and feel weak and by the time you get in the ring you are already beat. I have seen it. On the other hand nerves are a natural thing and I've suffered with them but healthily. The mental aspect plays a big part in the fight game and I would say it's as much as 70% because it's not just during the fight or before the fight, it's the build up to the fight and anyone who has ever boxed at any level will know that. The mental aspect is a big thing.

# ROUND 4

# NEW HORIZONS

In the summer of 1998 I left the Army. They offered me a pre-release course and I never took it which I regret now. I had no plans and headed back to my Parents house until something came up. I had my HGV license and put my name down with an agency and went to the boxing gym to keep in shape.

I phoned my pal Billy who had also just came out of the Army and asked him if there was anything happening anywhere and he asked me to go down to Portsmouth where he lived and we'd do a bit of agency driving and see what else was about. I had been back at my Parents house about a month and didn't want to be under their feet so I took Billy up on his offer and off I went to Pompey.

We signed on the dotted line with an agency to be drivers and we were just scratching about living off a little savings that were disappearing at an alarming rate. Then Billy said something which really got my attention. He said he knew a man in Hartlepool called Graham who said he would get us a place to live and pay us to fight for his club. He mentioned a couple of ABA champions who were at the club, both of whom I knew, and we could do a bit of driving work. There were no other offers on the table so what did we have to lose. It sounded too good to be true.

We got the coach from Portsmouth to London and then made the long old journey from London up to Hartlepool.

When we got there we made our way to Graham's house and he sorted us a nice hotel to stay in until he got us something more permanent. We hit the ground running and got straight into the party scene. We also done plenty of hard work in the gym as Graham had a big show in a few weeks and we were both on it, so we partied hard and we trained hard. We were both ex squaddies so this is what we were used to.

The show itself was jam packed and the support was amazing. You would think we were both Hartlepool born and bred the way we were welcomed with open arms by everyone. Billy had a good fight and beat Sheffield's Paul King on points.

I couldn't have had a harder opponent if I chose one myself. I fought a Lithuanian called Key Vsyniavskas (try saying that after a few beers). He'd had 23 fights in England and had won them all and was boxing for Parsons Cross gym in Sheffield. Apparently he was supposed to be living above the gym but if it was true or not I don't know. What I did find out when the bell rang was he came to win and was as tough as teak.

Paul Fraser wrote: "Bennett started off most brightly with a few good blows to his opponents head and as the fight went on it became a much closer bout before Bennett regained control in the final round. As a result of this he gained a split verdict with scores of 80-78 twice and 78-79."

We went toe-to-toe for four rounds in an absolute war. I was roared on by my new army of fans and was now an adopted Poolie. I said at the time "I was not fully aware of the fitness of my opponent and how strong he was, but, through brilliant coaches I got through."

My first impression of the gym at the Hartlepool Boys Welfare was that it had no soul. It wasn't like the boxing gyms I was used to, this one was in a sports hall and before every session all the punch bags had to be put up and the make shift boxing ring erected. The process repeated in reverse after every training session and you would never have thought boxing took place there. It was used for a variety of sports. That's why I thought it had no soul but it had been going like that for years and they'd produced a number of ABA champions.

The first time Graham took me on the pads he was talking in an American accent!

'Nice hook baby'

'Stick it baby' and things like that. I felt like an extra in a boxing film.

There was an ex-pro there called Neil who used to spar with all the lads, he took a shine to me and took me under his wing so to speak. As I got to know everyone involved with the club, boxers, coaches, families and fans, they were such a diverse group of people from all walks of life. There were a lot of 'characters', some would stab you in the back as soon as it was turned and others would give you the shirt off their back. You soon found out who was who, and who you could and couldn't trust. Some I hit it straight off with like I had known them for years and others I would just nod 'hello' to.

After one show down the country somewhere, the Police were called the next morning. One of the lads was still off his nut and was on the hotel roof in just his underpants, throwing roof tiles down and shouting 'Strangeways.'

Even the national England team coach said to me:

"You are in with a bad lot there Benny."

When I first arrived at the club my dyed blond hair was growing out so it looked like I had tips.

"Alright Tips"

"My name is Benny" I'd say.

Soon my hair grew out and 'tips' was never mentioned again.

We had a good strong team and were getting plenty of fights all over the country, Liverpool, Manchester, Sheffield, Coventry, Sunderland and all over Scotland.

I remember during one of our visits to Scotland, Michael Hunter was giving one of their top lads; who was a Scottish International, a going over and then let out a shout "He just bit me" and there was a bite mark on his shoulder. The ref told the lad not to do it again and the fight resumed. Not wanting it to end in disqualification, Mick gave him a pasting but kept his body parts away from the guy's jaws.

Ian Cooper, our ABA middleweight champ was boxing the heads off them all up there as well. The shows were billed as 'Scottish Select v England Select' but it was only our club, we were the England Select. People who had been involved in boxing for many years were left bewildered and saying "How can one small club from Hartlepool come up here and beat the best lads in Scotland?"

The reason was because we had a lot of quality in our squad, four ABA champions and three England Internationals, not bad for a little club.

I remember fighting a lad called George Telfer of O'Neill's ABC in Edinburgh. He was Scottish champ and supposed to be the next big thing and had an unbeaten record of 26-0 and was a knock-out specialist. The way the Scots talked about him you'd think I was there as a sacrificial lamb. As soon as the bell went I was on him and didn't give him any room. He came at me throwing shots because he was a come forward fighter, and every punch he threw I hit him with counters off the front foot and sank body shots in for good measure and I'm sure the crowd were shell shocked. This wasn't in the script. It was a cracking fight which received a standing ovation from the crowd who appreciated a quality fight when they saw one. I thought I won every round even though it was close and they took ages to announce the decision. I knew they were trying to take it away from me, but they finally saw sense and gave it to me by a majority and I couldn't help thinking it must have killed them to do that. I took their champion's unbeaten record.

Another fight I had was in Glasgow and was a barnstormer which got fight of the night. It was against another Scottish ABA champ called Michael Kirwin. It was a hard fight but I was never hurt and landed much more punches and again they took ages to announce the verdict. I won the fight but lost the decision on a majority and even some local Scottish fans voiced their opinion with shouts of 'cheating bastards'. I never let it bother me it's all part and parcel of the game. I fought another good lad up there whose name escapes me, he was a pretty decent fighter with a good reputation and knew his way around the ring but I out-boxed him and won on points. We all enjoyed our jaunts up in Scotland they were good times.

This was my final year as an amateur, as I'd made my mind up I was going pro after the championships, so this was my last assault on the ABA title and I wanted to go out as champion.

My first bout in the regional rounds was against a lad called Joe Donkin and I dropped him a couple of times and stopped him in the second round.

The next round was the big one, the one I'd been waiting for. It was against the defending ABA champion Nigel Wright who put me out of the competition the previous year and took my spot on the Commonwealth Games team. I was really fired up for this; it was the ABA final to me, I wanted to settle the score and get even. My pride was on the line. The thing about Nigel was he was a really good boxer and he could hit hard. He had great footwork and moved a lot and normally when you move a lot you don't have the power, but when he held his feet and let go he could bang. If you gave him room to box he would box your head off, he was a lovely boxer. I liked to throw my shots at mid-range and short-range and he liked to throw at long-range.

I learned my lesson from our first fight and jumped on him as soon as the bell rang. I didn't give him any room and forced him to hold a lot which resulted in him getting a couple of warnings, in fact he spent a lot of the four rounds holding, but I beat him fair and square and settled the score, it was a great feeling. The unanimous decision was scored 79-77, 79-76 and 78-75 in my favour.

After beating the champion I remember thinking my name was on the ABA title, because I couldn't see anybody who was left in the competition beating me.

I then became Northern Counties champion after dishing out a hammering to Malcolm McIvor, who got a couple of standing counts and I won 24-3 on the computer scoring.

The quarter-finals were in Coventry and I fought a very strong lad called Terry Adams who had the reputation as a big puncher. It was an easy fight for me and I out-boxed him quite-handily and won every round. His only success was a right hand in the last round and I was sporting a lovely shiner the next day.

Middlesbrough's defending ABA middleweight champ John Pearce went into the quarter-final with a badly damaged hand and should have pulled out. Even with one hand he put up a great fight and only lost by the narrowest of margins, a 3-2 split, to Carl Froch who went on to have a great career.

The Hartlepool fans were absolutely amazing and I'd never known a town love their boxing so much. To see and hear them in Coventry and everywhere else we fought was a big boost to us in the ring. So far I'd had four fights in the championships and had fought two boxers and two fighters so it was a good mix and I was confident my name was on the ABA title.

The semi-finals were held at the York Hall in Bethnal Green and I was up against a natural southpaw called Jon Honney, the other semi was between another two southpaws, Danny Happe and Stephen Yates. Happe won it in the first round.

I was next up and I didn't give Jon Honney time to think and was on him before the first bell died down, he tried to push me off but fell forward a little and I hit him with a right uppercut and a left hook and he was kissing the canvas. He beat the count but I was straight on him, bish, bash, bosh and he was down again and it was all over in 40 seconds. I was in the ABA final and I was buzzing. This was going to be my year. Not only was I in the final but so were two of my club mates, Michael Hunter and Billy Bessey. Hunter beat Anthony Gribben on points and Billy beat Bob Harding in the second round on cuts. James Rooney from the Catholic club lost a close decision to Steven Burke otherwise Hartlepool would have had four boxers in the ABA finals. Never before had anything like this happened in the history of the boxing mad town or never will it ever likely happen again. Not in my lifetime anyway. It felt like we were a unique part of history and it was fever pitch and excitement everywhere you went and that's all anybody wanted to talk about. Total strangers would pull me up in the street and want to talk about the upcoming big fights and strangers would shout well wishes and good luck messages to me. It was a really big thing in the town and they embraced it wholeheartedly.

What a great time it was for amateur boxing in Hartlepool, the full town was buzzing over it and we were never out of the local papers. It was a unique moment in the town's long history with amateur boxing to have three lads in the ABA finals. We were all up against the same club as well which made it even more unreal. We faced the mighty Repton Club from London, who were and still are the biggest amateur boxing club in Great Britain. Repton have a long history and have produced hundreds of ABA champions.

An army of fans from Hartlepool arrived in their droves as coach loads descended on the Barnsley Metro Dome on St. George's day April 23.

Michael Hunter beat Andrew Wallace by one point in a hum dinger to add the ABA bantamweight title to the ABA flyweight title he won two years previous. It was actually his third final in a row. He lost out at flyweight the previous year when making the weight limit was taking too much out of him.

My opponent Danny Happe, was a tall and rangy southpaw with lovely skills and it was over four rounds with the dreaded and controversial computer scoring system.

Boxing News Daniel Herbert previewed the finals and of my fight he said:

"This could be one of the best, a fascinating tactical battle between a stocky boxer with a compact defence in Bennett and a tall boxer enjoying the form of his life in Happe.

Bennett has a good international record. He was robbed against Denmark and then won in Ireland, within the space of eight days in March 1998, but perhaps the key lies in Kevin's improved form against southpaws.

Last year when he was still in the Army, he was eliminated at the quarter-final stage by Shildon southpaw Nigel Wright (the eventual champion), but this season unanimously outscored Wright in the Tyne, Tees & Wear final before destroying left-handed Jon Honney of Basingstoke in the semis.

Happe was also a one round winner in the semis, which suggests he is hitting with more authority. It should be close, but Bennett's tight defence can keep out the Londoner for a points win. Pick: Bennett."

I knew that if I jumped on him from the opening bell he wouldn't be able to hold me off and that proved to be the case. I hit him that many times in the opening two rounds I thought he might have retired on his stool. He was tough or he wouldn't have been able to take the hammering he was getting and he got another pasting in the third. I slowed down a bit in the last round because I'd put that much into the first three rounds and he caught me with a couple of jabs, but I still outworked him and won the round. I won every round and had won this by a landslide. I was ABA champion and was just waiting for official confirmation to crown me as champ. Then the announcement came 'The winner and 1999 ABA light-welterweight champion, by 9 points to 8, Happe', I was stunned and I thought they had announced it wrong. The crowd were in shock and people gasped in disbelief. Lots of people then started shouting 'robbing bastards'. I'll never forget it and it hurt me more than any punch I've ever taken in my life. You can sum it up in one word, Corruption. I hit him with over a hundred shots during the four rounds and only eight were scored, what a farce. One of my coaches went around some of the Repton team and asked who they thought won and every one of them said 'Bennett'. He even went up to the one of the national England coaches and asked him who he thought won and he said 'Bennett won hands down'.

A newspaper report said: "It looked like Bennett had won by a good margin. Happe hardly threw a punch in the first two rounds as Bennett built up a big lead. Late in the fourth round the Londoner finally connected with a couple of jabs and snatched a win he didn't deserve."

Danny Happe went on to win three ABA titles at three different weights and a Gold Medal at the Multi-Nations.

Billy Bessey knocked out Joe Young in the third round to win the Super-Heavyweight title. We would have had a clean sweep if it wasn't for the bent officials.

I was ready to turn professional, I'd had enough of the amateur game, I had boxed at the top level and there was nothing else I wanted to do but turn pro and try my hand there, but the England team called me up for the Multi-Nations, so I thought yeah ok I'll bow out as an England International, so I boxed in the 1999 Multi-Nations which were actually held in Liverpool which meant I didn't have to travel out the country.

I got a bye in the first round which put me straight through to the quarter-finals, so a win here would mean I was guaranteed a bronze medal. In the quarter-final I was up against the Danish champion; Mehmet Erarslan. I had fought this guy before in Denmark when I was captain of the England team and I thought I won with plenty in hand but they gave him the decision and even the headlines in the Boxing News said, 'Bennett Robbed in Denmark'. I saw this as a chance of getting even. Mehmet Erarslan was one of Denmark's most decorated boxers and the list of titles he had won was as long as my arm. I took no prisoners and punched him from pillar to post and won 16-3 on the computer scoring. I hit him with some solid shots and caught him clean a few times with the right uppercut. I will say one thing, he was very tough.

I was now in the semi-final and one win away from a Gold medal fight and you never guess who I was up against? None other than my old rival Nigel Wright. We had many hard rounds of sparring together at the England camp and our fight for a place in the final was no different. Nigel boxed on the back foot and I chased him and closed him down and moved forward constantly, it was a good fight. It could have gone either way but he got the decision 7-5 on the computer scoring. I came away with a Bronze medal at the Multi-Nations in my last amateur fight. That was it for me, the vest came off and I was ready to turn professional.

While I was still in Liverpool, before I went home from the Multi-Nations, I got a job to go sparring with the former Olympian David Burke who was in training for an important fight. David was a very good boxer, tall and rangy. I was down to spar six rounds with him but I cut him over the eye, I can't remember what round it was, and that was his preparation for the fight ruined. I bet he regretted inviting me to spar.

## PART TWO

## PROFESSIONAL BOXING CHAMPION

# ROUND 5

# PROFESSIONAL BOXER

I turned professional as a light-welterweight but thinking about it now, a few of us got our professional licenses at the same time and we became a 'new gym' at Neil Fannan's headquarters at Brierton in Hartlepool.

Ian Cooper turned pro and Neil Fannan got his trainer's license, Richy Horsley got his seconds license and Dave Garside took out a manager and promoters license. I didn't sign a contract with Neil or Dave it was a verbal agreement.

We were training hard with morning runs on the beach on Mon, Tue, Thurs, Fri, Sat, with gym work Mon through Friday. It was a lot of stamina work and more emphasis on power and sitting down on your shots. Instead of sitting on my back foot, I adjusted my weight so I was a little more over my front foot, slowed my footwork down a little and planted my feet more, although I'd always had a pro style so it didn't need that much tweaking. I sparred a lot with Ian Cooper who was a quality super-middleweight and a couple of stone heavier. It was a nice change when I got someone my weight to spar with when it was arranged for me to do some sparring with two-times ABA champion Alan Temple who was a seasoned pro. Alan Temple was brilliant in the sparring sessions and it was good experience, he was very clever and awkward and to tell you the truth, I had a bit of trouble with him; he was so sharp but it was just what I needed. I sparred with Alan a few times and also his stablemate Mo Helel, who was an old Boys Welfare club mate of mine. We also went to Middlesbrough while Ian Cooper sparred with John Pearce (two-times ABA Middleweight champion and Commonwealth Games Gold Medal 1998) and I done a few rounds with ABA champion Andy Green. It was all systems go.

Then we got the news we had been waiting for, our professional debuts were set for 1st December 1999 at a venue called Tall Trees in Yarm and the show sold out within a week.

On the evening of the fight we were all in a hotel room chilling out watching the 'Nutty Professor' on TV and we were rolling about laughing at it. One of the team who was an ex-pro champ, started to get ready for the show and when he took his trousers off his vest was tucked into his underpants. We all looked at each other and were in hysterics, couldn't breathe, faces purple, sides aching, what a scream. I've never laughed so much before a fight and I'll never forget it as long as I live.

Ian Cooper, roared on by the massive crowd, got off to a winning start and won a points decision over a journeyman called Martin Jolly. Then a bit of British boxing history was made when Jan Wild fought Audrey Guthrie. It was the first time that two British female professional boxers had fought each other, all the other times up to that point had involved a foreign opponent. Then Liverpool's Jason Vlasman outscored Mo Helel. Now it was my turn, I was the last fight of the night and didn't know I'd be in one of the hardest fights of my life.

It was only a 4 x 3 min round fight but those 12 minutes were like half an hour because in the other corner was Karim 'The Beast' Bouali. He looked a stone heavier but back then when you fought out of your area, you got a piece of paper with your weight on it and you took it with you to the show as proof of your weight, and he was fighting out of the Peacock gym in Canning town. I had to box this beast on the back foot, to stand and trade would have been suicidal, he was so tough and strong. Sometimes it felt like I was fighting for my life and the rounds felt like ten minutes long but I had to box like my life depended on it because he wasn't called the beast for nothing, he was relentless. I'd had a long amateur pedigree and fought every type of style at the highest level and it stood me in good stead. I pulled everything out in that fight and you can imagine how exciting it was, the crowd were going crazy and I was glad to hear the final bell and won a very close decision. I couldn't have had a harder fight for a debut and Ken Morton who covered it for Boxing News headlined his piece 'Kevin's Baptism of Fire'. Ken also said "Bennett boxed well in the opening two sessions, picking off an advancing opponent with short neat punches. The Marseille-born Bouali was hooking with both hands to the body, but Bennett, a lively addition to the pro ranks, kept his nose in front."

I remember saying to my trainer Neil: "If that is what pro boxing is all about, I wished I'd stayed amateur." Then I laughed as I was only a joking.

We never used that matchmaker again because he tried to stitch us up that night but we should have known he meant business because he booked a table for ten and they weren't coming all that way to watch their man lose, and not long after that night, Karim Bouali had a full page advert in the Boxing News issuing challenges to Ricky Hatton, Shea Neary, Junior Witter and Eamon Magee. What I thought was strange was Karim had another seven fights, all wins, and mysteriously never fought again. His last fight was a ninth round knock-out win for the WBU International light-welterweight title. Maybe he fell out of love with the game when he couldn't get the big fights, like Hatton and Witter, because nobody wanted a piece of him. It's a shame really because he had a big future ahead of him in my opinion.

Just after Christmas about half a dozen of us went on a lad's holiday to Tenerife to celebrate the Millennium, which included some of my England amateur team mates David Haye and Audley Harrison. I was in a twin room with Audley Harrison for the week and one night when we were painting the town red, I wasn't feeling too good so I went back to the hotel room for an early night, hoping I would feel better in the morning. I was woken up during the night by the sound of the key in the door and in walked Audley with a woman. The strange thing was they didn't put the light on and were sat talking on the end of the bed while I was laid still and not making a sound a few feet away. Audley went to the toilet and left the woman sat on the bed and she didn't move or attempt to put the light on, I couldn't believe she didn't know I was there so I stayed still and was laid there like a sniper. Audley came back in the room and she went to the bathroom and while she was in there he switched the light on and got the shock of his life when he saw me! During a brief exchange of hushed words I told him I wasn't going anywhere and he quickly switched the light off. As my eyes adjusted to the darkness I could only see the outline of shadowy figures making groaning noises and Audley talking in a Barry White like voice, 'Oh yeah baby', 'That feels good baby', and all the rest of it. I swear to god my body was jerking all over as I was trying not to laugh out loud. That woman didn't even know I was there. The lads pissed themselves laughing when I told them the next day. The following summer life would change for Audley when he won a Gold Medal at the Olympic Games and signed a big money television deal which made him a millionaire.

Meanwhile there were no such luxuries in my life and it went on as normal. I was in between fights and there wasn't any on the horizon so I took a job working away for a couple of weeks. We were outdoors in the freezing temperatures doing curtain walling and some of us rented a flat. One of these nights I went out for a run, I didn't really want to go but I didn't want to lose too much fitness so off I went in the Antarctic conditions and got lost. I eventually found my way back and wasn't in a great mood but the warm flat made me feel much better, now for a nice hot bath and something to eat. I ran the bath and all that came out was cold water, the other lads had been in the bath and run all the hot water off so I had to have a cold wash. Then I went in the fridge to get my food out and it was gone, all that was left was a scabby looking jacket potato and a bit of butter. Richy was sat at the kitchen table tucking into what looked like my food!

"Richy you're eating my fuckin' scran" I said in a not so friendly voice. He looked at the food on his plate, then looked in the open fridge while not getting up from the chair and said "Aw you know what I might have done!"

He said he thought it was his and took it by accident but I reckon he looked in the fridge and seen the choice and didn't fancy his much so ate mine while I was out running.

I was soon in the gym with a fight coming up and Dave Garside starting promoting Sunday afternoon boxing shows at Seaton Carew. The atmosphere at these sold out shows are some of the best I've ever experienced.

I fought Les Frost from Doncaster. He had a skinhead but didn't look too ferocious; he had a little go in the opening half minute but couldn't cope with my power and I dropped him at the end of the first but the bell saved him. I didn't waste any time in the next session and a lovely left hook finished him and the 500-strong crowd brought the house down.

I said to sports journalist Roy Kelly: "If a quick win comes along then brilliant, but it doesn't always happen that way. I think I have come on a lot since my debut, but I didn't get the chance to show it because it was over early but I'm over the moon with the performance."

My trainer Neil Fannan also said: "Benny was a very good amateur but professional boxing is a business. If he can get the job done early and get out without suffering any damage then that is much better. He's improving and we're very happy with him. Even when he was trying to destroy Frost, Benny never once disregarded his defence. One of the assets he boasts is that he has never been put down. Not many fellas can boast at having over 100 fights and never having seen the canvas."

One of the Hartlepool pro's called James Rooney was being managed by a man called Mick Marsden from Leeds, who had just secured a Sky TV contract. There was an opportunity for me to sign with him so I spoke to Neil and Dave who told me to go ahead with it, so I went to Leeds with Neil and spoke to Mick Marsden. He told me about the Sky TV deal and how I could be involved with fights on the live shows. It was agreed I'd have a fight for him and we'd take it from there and talk some more so I signed for him.

Before I fought for him he phoned up with some sparring work in Leeds and said Derek Roche was looking for some sparring as he had a fight coming up, I said yes I'll do it. Roche had just lost the British Welterweight title, and his unbeaten record, in his last fight against Harry Dhami and was determined to regain it. I thought it would be excellent to spar with someone of his experience and quality and hoped I would take something away from the sparring. Roche was a come forward fighter and very tough and we did six hard rounds. The first round was about thirty seconds old when I threw a left hand feint and put a right hand straight down the pipe which landed flush and wobbled Roche badly. He soon shook it off but I knew I had gained his respect. It was a really good experience for me and I got a lot of confidence from it because I did so well.

My third pro fight and my first for Mick Marsden, was at Pontefract against Steve Hanley. I had sparred with Steve when I was a kid in the West Midlands when we both boxed for Warley, he was a few years older than me and gave me something of a pasting back then which I hadn't forgot, this was my time for revenge. There were loads of fans that made the trip from Hartlepool and all were singing and shouting my name, it was a good feeling. I couldn't believe how tough Steve Hanley was, I couldn't remember him being this tough and by tough I mean he soaked up a lot of punishment and hung in there. I hit him with some big shots and he took them and stayed on his feet. I hammered him with bone shuddering body punches and crisp head shots and dominated the six rounds but couldn't put him away and won a unanimous decision.

Then I fought on another awesome Sunday afternoon show in Seaton Carew against a really dangerous puncher called Gary Reid, who I had outpointed in the amateurs. He had a left hook like Joe Frazier and if it landed it would knock you into next week. I boxed him in the first round and had a look at him, I dropped him in the second but the bell saved him. I was told between rounds not to get too excited and stick to my boxing which is what I did in the third. He came for me in the fourth and was looking to land the big shots but I caught him and dropped him. He got up and didn't seem to know where he was but the ref allowed it to continue, so I steamed in and was hitting him with unanswered punches and the ref stopped it. Reid didn't protest and walked unsteadily back to his corner.

Extracts from John Jarrett's report in Boxing News said:

"Kevin Bennett hit too hard and too fast for Wolverhampton warrior Gary Reid. Kevin put his shots together well and in the second round, as Reid swapped punches, Bennett threw a left-right and a short right uppercut and Reid fell on his face. He got to his feet and the bell rang. In a good third round they tested each other with solid punches. In the fourth round a cracking right to the head sent Reid down on his back. He beat the count but was shaken up as Bennett went in to finish the job. With Reid under fire, the referee called it off."

My trainer Neil Fannan was speaking to Richard Jacques and said:

"Benny worked really hard to get on top and then finished it off really well. He is improving all the time and I am delighted with his progress. He is already two-thirds up the British ratings but it's existing in the last third that is important."

# ROUND 6

# THE SKY IS THE LIMIT

Next up was my first fight live on Sky TV like Mick had promised me, and it was at the Coventry Sky Dome against Gary Harrison. I was paid a lot more money for this live Sky TV fight which was a bonus as my girlfriend Gemma and I had moved in a flat together. Harrison looked the next weight division up and was quite big, but I chopped him down to size with some wicked body punches. I got into a rhythm quickly and mixed it to head and body and dropped him at the bell to end the second round, he'd decided he'd had enough and never came out for the third. My trainer Neil was happy and he said I made Harrison look ordinary. Top of the bill was Richard Evatt against Roy Rutherford and what a great scrap it was.

My next fight was on another Sky show against the journeyman Keith Jones, who just came to survive and covered up and I won every round for a unanimous decision. At the end of the millennium I was 6-0 with 3 KO's as a pro.

My first fight of 2001 was at the Crawley Leisure Centre and was live on Sky against Liverpool's Tommy Peacock. I knew Tommy from the amateurs he had a really good pedigree and boxed for England. I didn't see him much on the domestic scene he was mainly an International fighter and he had a terrific left hook.

Tommy won his first 12 and then lost to Ricky Hatton for the Central Area title, and then lost again so I think he was at a bit of a turning point in his career. We both had black shorts and neither of us wanted to change so our camps had to toss for it and he won. I didn't have a spare pair of shorts in my bag so I had to wear a pair of white ones with Sky wrote on them. I was more than a little narked over it and when he won the toss he looked a bit smug about it and that pissed me off so I had a bit of a bee in my bonnet. I didn't help my cause as I was charging in too much in the first few rounds but I was winning them comfortably enough. I was putting power into every shot instead of relaxing and letting my boxing do the work. He was constantly holding and trying to frustrate me and forever rabbit punching me behind the head, which we all know is an illegal punch in the rule book. He even threw me to the floor once when it was getting a bit messy. I was the aggressor throughout the first four rounds and had him rocking on a few occasions.

The fifth round was about 15 seconds old when we clinched again and he was holding and hitting me behind the back of the head. To say it was annoying would be an understatement. I managed to get my arm free and swung a right hook over which connected flush on his jaw and he was out before he hit the floor, he hit the canvas with a sickening thud and his head bounced a few times. The referee Larry O'Connell showed his great experience by stopping it immediately and the paramedics were inside the ropes within seconds and had the oxygen mask straight on Tommy and worked on him. After a few minutes he thankfully came round. At that stage I wasn't looking at him as a man I was fighting, but looking at him as a fellow man.

He was married with kids and I was so pleased to see he was alright. The referee congratulated me after it for my professionalism.

I couldn't have asked for a deadlier right hook than that, it was a brutal finish and it was in the 2001 best knockouts. Defeating Tommy was a good scalp for me because he was no mug and had an excellent pedigree so I was happy with that win and got rated at number 12 in Great Britain at light-welterweight.

My manager Mick Marsden said: "Benny has come far very quickly but he has only had seven contests and the guys around him are well into double figures. In one way he is a grown man and you can't slow him down, but I want him to keep learning as he's going because this is an exciting division. I'm proud of Benny and the way he knocked out Peacock."

My life was soon about to change because after the Peacock fight, my girlfriend Gemma told me she was pregnant and I was overjoyed I was going to be a father.

Another massive addition to my life came in the shape of a Staffordshire bull terrier that my parents had bred and promised me pick of the litter. The litter consisted of three brindle bitches and two white dogs and I picked the dog with the dark brindle patch over his eye, as soon as I saw him I knew he was the one. When he was six weeks old we went down to the Midlands to bring him home to Hartlepool and I called him Hagler after my favourite boxer Marvellous Marvin Hagler. Gemma was working in the Dentist's at the time so when I wasn't training, I was with Hagler and he was a little beautie. I was out walking him one day when he was still only a pup and we were in an old cemetery that had a small wall on one-side and an eight foot drop on the other. He was off the lead and ran and jumper over the wall and I saw him disappear and I thought the worst. I looked over and he was laid on his side and I thought he'd broken a leg or something. I picked him up and carried him home and put him in the car and went to the vets. When I opened the car door he jumped out happy as Larry and back to normal, he had only winded himself the little rascal. He was a character and was in many scrapes over the years. Another time when Gemma and I had moved into our first house, he just went missing, vanished from under our noses. We looked all over for him to no avail so we phoned around vets in the town and one of them said a dog matching the description had been treated by them. They said the dog had been run over by a bus and if he hadn't have been the breed he was and as tough as he was, he would have been killed. He had a damaged leg and the hair never grew back on it but it wasn't broken. The dog was in the care of the Police and that's where we went to get him back.

I bred him once and got pick of the litter and picked a white dog and called him Duran. As Duran got older he was challenging Hagler to be top dog and they were constantly fighting and some of the fights were really vicious. Once when we went down the Midlands to see my parents we asked Gemma's dad to pop round and feed the dogs. We told him to feed them separately and definitely not together, which he must have forgot about because I got a frantic phone call at my parent's house, Gemma's dad was in a panic and couldn't split them up so I had to dash home three hours away which was a long drive and felt more like six. When I got back both dogs were covered in blood. Duran's face was full of bite marks and scars and Hagler's leg had been chewed and he was limping. I cleaned them both up and got them the right medicine and they soon got better but I realised I couldn't keep them both and one of them had to go, so I found Duran a new home.

Talking about white dogs brings back a memory of a dog we had when I was a kid. We called the dog Sam and he was a Rhodesian ridgeback cross, we had him from a pup until he died of old age when he was about 15. He was white and had a smooth coat and was built like Hercules. He was a beast and the strength of that dog was immense. I spent most of the time with him and fed him, cleaned up after him, took him for walks and exercised him, so although there were seven of us in our house (parents and five kids) he was practically my dog.

Everyone was trashed of him, even the neighbours, and if he ever got out they would phone our house to say the dog was out and nobody would venture outside until he was back indoors. He was intimidating to look at so people automatically thought he was a devil dog but he wasn't. He was great with other dogs but he hated cats. I took him out for a walk one day, I was around nine or ten years old, and he saw a cat and shot off after it. Only thing was I had hold of the lead and wouldn't let go and he dragged me along the street and over the road and only stopped when the cat jumped a fence and a wall and he realised the chase was futile.

My face was cut and grazed and covered in blood and when I got home and told my dad what had happened he said 'Here Son' and put his hand in his pocket (I thought he was going to pull a fiver or a tenner out) and he gave me one pence and said: "Well done for holding on to him." I didn't find it funny at the time but thinking about it now I can't stop laughing; it was just my dad's dry sense of humour.

I got myself back into training and was going to Champs Gym in Manchester sparring with the former British lightweight champion Wayne Rigby, who had a World title fight coming up. We had a few hard sparring sessions which was good for both of us. Rigby was at a very good level so it was a bit of a learning curve for me because I wanted to be where he was. Wayne was really tough and game and I would say our spars were evenly matched and we both got something out of them.

My next fight was against Watford's Ian Eldridge at the Wembley Conference Centre. I was in better shape than I was against Peacock and felt confident and couldn't wait to get in there. I didn't box to plan in the first few rounds of the Peacock fight and was rushing in and loading up and didn't get my shots off as I would have liked, so I didn't want to make that mistake against Eldridge. I knew he was a bit of a banger who was coming to have a go and he had only lost one fight and was ambitious like me. I liked taking on fighters like that it made me sharper. A strange thing happened in this fight because I broke his nose with my head! He was taller than me and a come forward fighter and as he came in, I stepped in at the same time and my head caught him on the bridge of the nose and broke it. His nose bled profusely from then on and my jab was moving the red around his face as if it was a paintbrush. We both ended up caked in claret, it was a bloodbath but all the blood came off him. The broken nose might have taken him off his game plan but it was a pure accident. After six rounds I won 59-56 on referee Jeff Hinds scorecard. Eldridge's face looked like a Butcher's block after the fight.

I wanted to fight more regular and grew frustrated because I wasn't getting the fights, there wasn't any continuity and I was left twiddling my thumbs, which was not good for a prospect on the fringe of the top ten. I wasn't making big money like World champs who can only fight twice a year so I got a driving job to pay the bills and keep my head above water.

My next fight was live on Sky in the nightmare arena Barnsley Metrodome. I call it that because it was where I was blatantly robbed in the ABA final. Top of the bill was Tony Oakey, the lad whose eye I closed in sparring all those years ago at a weekend's training in East Anglia. My original opponent pulled out and I fought an old foe, the journeyman from Wales Keith Jones. I had him in trouble a few times and gave him a good hiding for six rounds. Jones trainer said to me afterwards "I thought you were going to stop him there." Nobody stopped Keith Jones and he had the awkward southpaw style that made good fighters look bad. He made a noise whenever he threw a shot and when I hurt him, he went into a shell and covered up and was hard to hit clean. He'd had well over 100 fights but I won every one of the six rounds and was now 9-0.

My next fight was in an eight round chief support, in a live Sky fight held at the Borough Hall in my adopted hometown of Hartlepool. It was the first time the Sky TV cameras had been to Hartlepool so you could say they were here because of me. I was up against Liverpool's Gary Ryder who was also unbeaten like me. The weigh-in was the day before and the fight was made at 10st 2lb and I came in at 10st 1lb and he weighed 10st 4lb. They told him to get the weight off and come back but he never even attempted to and weighed the same when he got back on the scales. They knew they had Sky by the balls and told them if they weren't happy to go and get someone else because they were leaving. We were almost bullied into taking it and had no choice. Thirty hours later when we got in the ring, people thought the wrong opponent had gotten in because Ryder looked massive and more like a middleweight.     Leading up to this I got a high protein and carb loading diet sheet, but I didn't follow it to plan and didn't put the weight back on like I should have. I felt drained and weak and had no energy.

I remember hitting him with a body shot in the second round and knew I'd hurt him but he took it well and kept coming. I dominated him and boxed his head off for six rounds and just ran out of gas, I had nothing left in the tank. I didn't rate Ryder; he didn't hit hard and never hurt me once. I was too good for him in all departments. I just blew out of steam because of the diet.

A magazine article (no author's name) said: "The Hartlepool fans had given Bennett a rapturous welcome and gave him sympathetic applause afterwards."

My manager Mick said it was a good learning fight for me and I would be back a much better fighter because of it.

My friend Billy Bessey won a four round decision over Nottingham's Gary Williams on the same bill and said: "That win was for Benny, he's my pal and I'm absolutely gutted for him, but he'll bounce back."

It was my first defeat and first set back but it came at a bad time because I was falling out of love with boxing. I wasn't getting the fights regular and there wasn't much money in it. Boxing wasn't delivering what I thought it would. Gemma was due to give birth to my baby daughter and there was no money in the pot and I was giving it some serious thought about retiring. I was sharing dressing rooms, and on the same shows, with lads who had 'made it' but after speaking to them, I realised they were still in the same boat as me. Where was the money going?

I had four months off and in that time I became a father when Gemma gave birth to our first born daughter, Keeley. It was an unbelievable feeling being a dad and I loved it and was proud as punch showing her off to everyone. My dog Hagler took to her straight away and he wouldn't leave her side, he stood guard over her. After those precious months with my new born daughter, I started to think about the fight game again and the only reason I didn't retire was because I still had a point to prove.

# ROUND 7

# AT THE CROSSROADS

When I was a kid starting out at Warley ABC, there were two brothers called Mark and Paul Ramsey who boxed for the Small Heath club. Both were brilliant amateurs and England Internationals and both won the ABA lightweight title. Mark won it in 1989 and Paul two years later in 1991. They both turned pro and the two of them ended up as journeymen pros. You know sometimes things don't work out as you plan them, but these two brothers were seriously talented amateurs and both gave Ricky Hatton all the trouble he could handle in pro fights. Paul almost stopped him on a bad cut but lost on points. The reason I mention these guys is because my next two fights were against them.

Paul fought under the name Paul Denton as a pro, because someone else had the same name so he used his mother's name, and I boxed him at the Mountbatten Centre in Portsmouth. He gave a lot of people problems and was a solid pro. I cut him in the third round and it was a good work out for me and just what I needed. I won every round on the referee's scorecard and was happy with the win.

Then I was due to fight the 'Brixton Barber' Ted Bami in Glasgow, but he pulled out because he had entered a barbering competition! The replacement was Mark Ramsey. He was experienced and clever and nobody dropped or stopped him but I dropped him with a right hand. He got up and recovered and he came at me and had a go. He certainly came to fight but I picked him off with counter-punches and won on points over six rounds. A cutting I have with no authors name on it said: "Bennett boxed neatly behind a high guard and with discipline. Bennett out-boxed the veteran clearly behind a stiff jab and sharp two and three punch volleys to collect referee Al Hutcheon's 60-54 verdict."

We were trying to get a fight with Young Mutley, I rated him, he was very dangerous and a good puncher. I fought him twice as an amateur and beat him both times. We made them three offers and each time the answer was no.

I went with Gemma and Keeley down to my parents for Christmas and enjoyed kicking back with my family. I only had a couple of drinks in that time and kept the discipline as I had a big fight coming up in January. I was back running on the beach as soon as I got home.

After the Christmas and New Year festivities, at the back end of January, I fought Glenn McClarnon over eight rounds live on Sky. He was rated number 8 in Great Britain and had won 12 out of 14 and one of those losses was on points over 12 rounds in a bid for the IBO Inter-Continental title. He looked massive compared to me and he was very strong. We fought eight really good quality rounds and after six I knew I was winning it. I was tired in the final round and thought the fight was a bit close for comfort, there was only a Rizla paper between us, but I thought I had done enough to win and as I went over to the ref for him to raise my hand, he raised Glenn's instead. He went forward more than me, I paced myself a little and didn't work as hard as I should have and that's what cost me it. Afterwards the ref told me it was all on the last round and there was nothing in it, but he had to choose a winner. Featherweight champ Nicky Cook and his dad told me they thought I won. It was a set-back but it wasn't the end of the world and I remember not being that bothered about it. It was a job, a serious business, unlike the amateur game. It was fun in the amateur's and no big deal if you lost, but in the pro game there was no fun and no money in it.

In between all the training, I was driving a taxi and also driving a 17 ton truck part-time to make ends meet. I was going months without a fight and when you're not fighting you're not earning. I wasn't getting the fights I needed and the fights I wanted, there was no consistency in my career, so again I was out of pocket and when I was fighting I wasn't earning enough money, so I was getting pissed off and losing interest.

I was training in the gym five days a week and running five days a week and I can't remember a day that I didn't wake up and wasn't aching. It took its toll on your body. I didn't have a nutritionist like they do now, I couldn't afford one. A nutritionist would have helped me with my diet so I was putting the right foods in to recover better and make weight better. Your body doesn't have time to recover when you are training like that and you are also trying to make weight, so I wasn't eating the right foods and I wasn't eating enough food. It was a vicious circle and I felt more like a weight-watchers champion than anything else.

A lot of prospects start out thinking they are going to earn a fortune, but when you get your pay cheque it's not as much as you think it's going to be. You have a prospect who is a floater at a live TV or Sky show, he is gloved up and ready, he could be gloved up for hours because none of the fights have ended early, and by the time he gets in the ring there's hardly anyone left in the arena. That's what happens when you are a floater. It can also work the opposite way and the fight ends early and they say you are on in five minutes.

Four months later I got my next fight and it was a big one against 17-0 Colin Lynes, it was on the undercard of British featherweight legend Naseem Hamed and this turned out to be Naseem's last fight, but by now I wasn't feeling it and wasn't motivated.

Colin Lynes was the name fighter and I was the opponent. I had seen him box as an amateur, Nigel Wright beat him in the ABAs, but I never really followed his pro career and wasn't unduly worried about him. Before the fight I just wasn't there mentally, I couldn't be bothered.

In the dressing room I was talking to a fighter called Jim Betts who was really nervous and I was trying to calm him down with some words of wisdom. I wasn't nervous one little bit.

The fight started and I didn't get going at all, I was lethargic. I boxed like I wasn't interested. Lynes was too sharp and I couldn't get my shots off and everything I tried to do he seemed to catch me. I never usually marked up but I was getting marked up pretty easily. His punches were stinging and he was catching me with everything. This wasn't the real Kevin Bennett; I was just going through the motions and it was like that every round. Colin wasn't known as a puncher but he dropped me in the fourth round and it was the first time I'd ever been down in 120 fights amateur and pro. It was just a flash and I was on the floor, I wasn't hurt I was in shock and jumped straight back up. He came at me throwing leather and I was punching back but the ref stopped it. I protested the stoppage and walked back to my corner feeling dejected. It should never have been stopped, but saying that, I was never going to win, not on that day. It was a bad day and it was the worst I've ever felt before, during and after any fight.

When you are a footballer and you have a bad game, they just say you've had a bad game and that's it, but you can't have a bad game as a boxer.

I was out the sport for ten months and for the first month or so I told myself I was retired. After a few months I started to think about boxing again. I was at the crossroads in my career. I knew I hadn't fulfilled my destiny by winning a pro title and felt a bit cheated.

I had a talk to my trainer Neil and he wanted me to come back and reinvent myself as a lightweight. I wasn't too keen on the idea at first because I struggled to make light-welterweight so I thought making the lightweight limit would kill me. The more I thought about it the more it made sense, a renewed chance for boxing glory in the lower weight division. It would mean slimming down without losing my strength. This was going to be a sacrifice I had to make so I had to be really disciplined about it. It would mean more rounds sparring, more work in the gym and more miles on the road. I didn't want to get to a point in a few years and know I didn't give it my all because it would be a big regret I'd have to live with. I have always been dedicated and believed I had the talent. It wasn't going to be easy but the thing was I didn't really have a choice if I wanted to fulfil my destiny, I was out of options. If I wasn't going to make it at lightweight it would be all over. It was all or nothing, so I said let's give it a go. I was determined to do this and be a success.

My first fight at lightweight was against a journeyman in a four rounder just to ease me back in and shake some ring rust off. I got a good four rounds under my belt and felt good and I won on points. The four rounds were in the bank now. I was back.

My next fight was three months later! It was so frustrating for me and like I said before there was no consistency and the inconsistencies had nothing to do with me because I wanted regular fights.

I was training hard and my weight was good and I was feeling fit. I was doing lots of sparring with Michael Hall and Francis Jones. After one spar Francis got out and said to Neil Fannan: "I can't believe any lightweight will be as strong as Bennett." I also done some sparring in Manchester as that was where my next fight was.

I was on the undercard to World middleweight champion Sergio Martinez at Manchester's MEN Arena and I faced a Hungarian called Zoltan Surman who'd only lost one fight. He was ripped and looked the part; he was game and came to fight but I was looking forward to getting down to business and making a statement.

Roy Kelly's report said: "Two crisp jabs immediately jolted back the head of Surman and Bennett followed in with thumping rights and lefts to the body. He varied his attack successfully in the first round, connecting with a right hook and a right cross plus a right uppercut while still finding the target with a purposeful jab. In the second round Bennett landed a thunderous right that wobbled Surman, who was blowing hard by the end of the round from having been weakened by powerful body shots. In the third the Hungarian was wobbled by a hard right in his own corner. At the start of the fourth Suman sustained a serious cut left eye and the blood was pouring onto the canvas and referee Mr Edwards stopped it. The end could have come at any time given the pressure Surman was under."

At the end of the third round I was sat on my stool and Neil said to me to go out and stop him and that was what I was about to do until he got a nasty cut.

Because I had been fighting bigger men, Surman wasn't strong enough for me and I dominated him. I felt strong and sharp and felt like my mojo was coming back. After I got out of the ring I was offered a big fight against Colin 'Dynamo' Dunne, the only thing was it was in two weeks!

I said I'd have to think about it but they wanted an answer there and then and offered me five grand so I said yes. Colin Dunne had lost his WBU World title by a split decision in his last fight and was looking for a 'warm up' fight before challenging for world honours again. If he beat me he had a crack at the IBO title lined up. I was his 'warm up' opponent. I knew this could be the opportunity I was looking for, all I had to do was beat Colin Dunne and it would throw a spanner in the works and I could be the one challenging for the title and then hopefully the money would come!

Neil said: "On Saturday against Surman I wanted him to go out and make a statement at lightweight and I think he did just that, he beat a good lad and I was well pleased. When Colin Dunne was World champion there was no bigger fan of his than me, but I think this is a great fight for Benny and one I'm confident he can win. Benny is a class fighter himself and this could be the big chance we wanted."

It was now down to me to produce the goods in the ring and my destiny was in my own two hands. Gemma had given birth to our second child eight weeks previous, a son we called Jake. I had a lovely wife, a daughter, a son and a dog. I felt like my family was complete and I was in a good place physically and mentally.

Standing next to Colin Dunne at the weigh-in he seemed tiny and I remember thinking to myself 'you can't beat me you're too small'. Remember I had come down from a higher weight division and was used to fighting men a lot bigger. I had watched lots of Dunne's title fights on the box; he was a very busy fighter and all action. After the weigh-in, Mick, Neil and I went for a walk in the July sunshine and had a chat. I felt good. I was back to my old self. I was ready.

The opening round started and we met in the middle and I stood my ground. Dynamo Dunne was straight into action and threw a few punches and I felt like they just bounced off me. I hit him with a couple of solid shots which seemed to jolt him. I felt strong and thought I may have been able to bully him. When the round ended I felt confident and so did my corner who said when I hit him I'd hurt him and to 'back him up in the next round'. In round two I caught him with a right hand, I didn't think it hit him flush but it did some damage and he hit the deck. When he got back up his legs had gone and I thought it would be stopped but the ref gave him every opportunity to recover. The ref waved it to continue and I knew Dunne was gone, so I went straight in for the kill and the first left hook dropped him and this time the ref waved it off. That win changed the direction of my career. I went from the lowest I'd ever felt and wanting to retire, having almost a year off and coming back as a lightweight to reinvent myself and give it one last go, to having three fights and putting myself in line for a shot at a title. Now we were talking about a title fight. I was on cloud nine.

A nice touch was in Tony Connolly's ringside report: "It was Kevin's biggest win and puts him right in the lightweight title picture. Dunne and trainer Colin Lake are two of the nicest guys in the sport and went over to congratulate Bennett and his coach Neil Fannan."

A family man, Kevin saluted his victim while watching a re-run of the finish. "It's a shame it had to end like that for him; he's a gentleman, one of my heroes. I almost wanted him to recover."

# ROUND 8

# FULFILLING A DREAM

I didn't have a high enough ranking to fight for the IBO World title but I still got a title fight only it was for the Commonwealth belt. If I won the Commonwealth title I would get the ranking which would qualify me to fight for the IBO championship which was the main goal.

I started training for a shot at the African Michael Muya. I had never seen any of his fights and didn't know anything about him, all I knew was he stood between me and fulfilling a dream of winning a professional title, a dream I'd had since I was a kid.

When I started sparring I sparred with who was available and looking back on it, nobody fit the bill of Muya. The lads I sparred were all strong lads a bit heavier than me. A typical days training consisted of an early morning run, stretching off first. Some days we'd run five miles and other days we would run ten miles. We'd also do a lot of beach running and we'd also run over the sand dunes to build the legs and stamina. Some gym sessions could go on for two hours, skipping, shadow boxing, pad-work with Neil wearing the body bag so I could practice whacking the body shots in. Then I'd do some rounds on the punch bags and then a few short sharp weights to build strength and finish off with abdominal exercises and the medicine ball.

On sparring days I'd spar 12 rounds and sometimes we would go to Leeds, Manchester and Liverpool for quality sparring. I would spar with one guy for two rounds, then he would get out and another would get in for two rounds, then another, and I would stay in for 12 rounds. Everything was going brilliant and I was in tremendous shape.

Mick Marsden said: "We don't know much about Muya, but we will give him the respect a champion deserves. Benny is looking bang on in training and we are confident he will win the title."

I told sports journalist Roy Kelly: "I will be boxing for Hartlepool. Hartlepool is my town now, it is where my missus is from and where my children were born and going to be brought up. I am proud of where I am from and am not turning my back on Oldbury. But when my name is announced I will be representing Hartlepool and this is where I intend to bring the belt the next day. There are no mixed loyalties, I feel very honoured boxing for Hartlepool – I love the place."

Ten days before the fight I had my last 12 round sparring session with two quality champions in Young Mutley, British welterweight champion and Ali Nuumbembe, Commonwealth welterweight champion. One of them would do two rounds and get out while the other got in and done two rounds and we'd repeat the process for 12 rounds. During the 10th round, Young Mutley caught me with a good shot on the nose and I felt it go and knew instantly it was broke. It never hurt but I turned and looked at my trainer and manager with a gutted look on my face because I thought the fight would be called off and my title shot was out the window. My nose was pouring with blood but I was told to carry on until the end of the round, which I did. I got cleaned up and went to get out the ring but they told me to spar the last two rounds! Can you believe it, I didn't get the point and still don't. My eyes were swelling up black and my broken nose was pissing blood non-stop but I finished the last two rounds and to say I was pissed off was an understatement. I put ice on my face every day to help with the swelling and I couldn't eat or drink properly because I was making weight and I felt really low.

Everything was kept quiet about my broken nose because the fight would have been called off and I couldn't pull out because I needed the money. The first time I laid eyes on Michael Muya was at the weigh-in and he was 6ft tall! The biggest lightweight I've ever seen, he looked like a young Thomas Hearns. I wore make up to hide my black eyes, I know it sounds ridiculous but it's true. I knew my nose would go as soon as it got hit but I thought as soon as it goes, I wouldn't feel it because I'd be pumped with adrenaline, but unless anyone has fought with a broken nose they'll never understand how hindering it is. I've watched fights since and as soon as they get a broken nose it gets stopped or the corner pulls them out, especially over 12 rounds and I went into the fight with a broken nose.

Muya hit me with a jab in the second round and my nose went and wouldn't stop pouring with blood from that moment. In between rounds my cut man was putting cotton buds soaked in adrenaline solution up my nose, which you are not supposed to do as it's strictly for cuts because it congeals the blood. It was congealing the blood at the back of my nose and blocking my air waves and as the fight progressed I was swallowing lots of blood. I totally out-boxed Muya for the first nine rounds and I buckled his legs with a right hand in the fourth, but the effects of the congealed blood blocking my air waves began to catch up with me and my brain was being starved of oxygen, so I can't remember the last three rounds. I can't remember what round it was maybe the ninth, when Neil was telling me to suck it up and win it for my children. I didn't know where I was and my face was a mask of blood with two eyes peeping through, how I got through it I'll never know and I was given oxygen in my corner after the fight but I have no memory of it.

In the dressing room I was given the Commonwealth belt but I thought I'd lost and they were giving me it out of sympathy so I threw it on the floor! I started to throw up and was taken to hospital to get checked over. They gave me a kidney dish and I was sick in it and filled it up five times with dark red blood that looked like black bean sauce, I've never been able to have black bean sauce on anything ever since.

I was put on a drip and was laid there with a broken nose and two black eyes and I was the winner!

I looked like I'd just opened a letter bomb!

My calves were cramping up with dehydration but I was starting to come to my senses again and less delirious and I couldn't help thinking about what I was putting my family through and remember thinking to myself 'is it all worth it'. Then my wife and parents came in and brought the title belt with them. I had my missus Gemma worried sick. She had always been there for me throughout my pro career and had been brilliant, putting up with me and my moods, and believe me that wasn't easy, especially when I had to make weight.

My trainer Neil made everyone laugh when he was telling people: "They were going to keep Benny in overnight but when they heard his patter they kicked him out after two hours."

I have got to include this great piece of reporting by Roy Kelly. Roy had covered my fights since I landed in Hartlepool in 1998 and I always had a good professional relationship with Roy, he has always been an honest and decent bloke. Here is the report from Roy Kelly:

"Kevin Bennett has added his name to the annals of Hartlepool sporting history by becoming the town's fourth Commonwealth boxing champion.

Referee John Keane scored it 116-113 to the man aptly known as the Bulldog.

The score-line does not tell the story of the greatest night of Bennett's life and the greatest fright of his life. It was an amazing story of skill and bravery beyond the call of duty.

Bennett appeared to be en-route to a comfortable points victory having boxed cleverly against the 6ft tall champion.

Going into round nine, the final third of the fight, it looked like Bennett would win in convincing fashion to achieve his dream of winning a major boxing title. However, what happened next would give the bout, which was already a fascinating clash of styles and size, the most dramatic and heart-stopping of climaxes.

There was little indication of the drama to come in that ninth as Bennett scored well, as a left-right combination and a couple of crisp right-handers kept him firmly in the driving seat.

While not a Rocky-style confrontation, it was certainly entertaining, and the Bulldog boxed the right fight against surely the tallest lightweight in the world.

Muya was a good mover but brought little to the contest except a smooth, yet harmless left hook, a sweet right uppercut and the punch at the end of round nine that seemed to make Bennett's legs dip just for a moment. It did not look of great significance at the time, but it was the first indication that all was not right.

Bennett came out for round ten in a lively fashion but two right uppercuts late in the round from Muya found their target. Bennett was not downed but struggled back to the blue corner looking absolutely shattered.

There followed the most vital eight minutes of his boxing career. The first sixty seconds were noteworthy for the decisive contribution by Coach Neil Fannan and manager Mick Marsden. Bennett indicated he could not continue, bringing an uncompromising riposte from his corner. Both Fannan and Marsden, though polite gentlemen, delivered some choice language they would not normally use around their Aunts for Sunday tea. Marsden physically grabbed the Bulldog and threw him out for the 11th.

Had it not been for their intervention, allied to a display of tremendous bravery from Bennett, he would have lost.

The 11th was all Muya, uppercuts from the right and left gloves, which were coated in Bennett's blood, hitting home, but the challenger refused to buckle. He was on automatic pilot, fighting on instinct and raw courage.

For the final three minutes, Bennett threw out his fists desperately so referee Keane could not call off the bout when in sight of the finishing line.

It was all hearts in mouth stuff as the 30 year old champion landed two right uppercuts and two left hooks, but miraculously Bennett, willed on by the sell-out crowd, stayed on his feet.

At the final bell both boxers embraced before looking to Mr Keane for the verdict and the Northampton official lifted the arm of Bennett. Justice was done, though there were no wild celebrations because the new champ had nothing left. He received oxygen on his stool and some expert medical care from Dr Fitzgerald.

After a worrying few minutes, Bennett left the ring to a huge ovation, including applause from the sporting Muya."

Neil Fannan said: "At the end of the tenth he told us he could not go on. I told him he had not lost a round and only had to stay on his feet to win. I reckoned he was at least six rounds up. Then at the end of the 11th I didn't give him a chance to say anything, I called him a lot of rude names and told him to go out for the last and win the title. He had been swallowing a lot of blood but had kept his boxing together nicely."

How dramatic was that report by Roy Kelly, absolutely brilliant and if I had been a spectator I would have loved to have been ringside for that one.

Robert Smith, Secretary of the British Boxing Board of Control and member of the Commonwealth Boxing Council said it was "one of the bravest performances I have seen for a long time. Kevin showed a tremendous amount of bravery and boxed very well against a very awkward champion."

A week later I was a guest on the Sky TV Ringside programme. I still looked like a panda with two black eyes but once the make-up team finished with me it looked like there was nothing wrong with me. I took the belt with me because they wanted to present it to me, as I never had it presented to me officially. They showed snippets of the fight and it was the first time I had seen it and I was a little embarrassed with the way I was stumbling about and it looked like a strong wind could have blown me over. The referee raised my hand and I nearly fell over. It's a funny thing when you've pushed your body to the absolute limits like that and sometimes it can be scary shit.

It was my schoolboy dream to one day win a professional title and now I had fulfilled that dream. You know something; I never truly felt the elation you should feel from winning something so significant. Sometimes realising your dream isn't quite what you envisioned.

Winning the Commonwealth title like that had a knock on effect and I was nervous about the distance and got demons about the 12 rounds. Although the Muya fight had been my first 12 rounder, I was having a psychological battle with myself because of how I struggled with 12 rounds, it was a mental thing.

My next fight was the big one for the IBO World title against Jason Cook, and to top it off it was in the same venue and same ring that I beat Muya for the Commonwealth belt in Bridgend, Wales.

I paced myself far too much and didn't work hard enough. It was a big clash between the best two lightweights in Great Britain and everyone thought it would be a thriller but the opposite happened. When I think about it I could kick myself because after 12 rounds I still had plenty left in the tank. You should leave it all in the ring and I never. The fight was winnable and I look at it as a missed opportunity but I only have myself to blame.

Gareth Jones reporting for Boxing News said: "It was close enough for there to be a degree of relief in the celebrations when MC John McDonald announced the result. Cook was the winner, but shared in the feeling of frustration that a showdown which promised much had been something of a damp squib."

I had lots of fights live on Sky, including title fights, and the money was still rubbish. People thought I was making a small fortune but that wasn't the case. I emphasized about the money from day one but got told "you can't be in it for the money, you've got to be in it for the glory and if you get the glory, the money will come".

I'm a realist and to me the glory was winning the title and when I won the title there was still no money. It doesn't filter out to everybody, there's no fair game in boxing. Money was my biggest gripe throughout my boxing career. 90% of boxers that people watched and looked up to will have full time jobs now. 90% of footballers you watch (and most of them couldn't hit a Cows arse with a shovel) will probably never have to work again in their lives. Money wise, the difference between boxing and other sports like football and golf is unbelievable. What you put yourself and your body through in boxing is second to none. You don't get the accolades and you don't get the rewards. If you look at the time between my fights, I wasn't making 15 grand a year and I paid 25% to my manager. That probably works out at around minimum wage, not exactly glitter and gold. It makes you fall out of love with the sport and you blame boxing because you are not getting the rewards, but really it's the people that run boxing. I would have carried on boxing if I could have afforded to but I had a wife and kids and had to think about them. If you did a survey of people who boxed all their lives and loved boxing, you would find that most of them quit because they couldn't afford to carry on. They have families and need to work a job and can't fit boxing into their lives. How sad is that. I don't want to sound hypocritical but I love boxing and I'll always love boxing, it's been in my blood since I was nine years old.

# ROUND 9

# DEFENDING CHAMPION

They say boxing is a lonely sport. When you are training, dieting and making weight it's a lonely sport. You are going through a lot of mental torture and nobody else is feeling it only you. I had struggled to make light-welter for years so making the lightweight limit killed me and I had to starve myself for days and go without water to dry out to make the weight. I had to go through this alone when everyone around me could eat and drink. It drives you mad and makes you feel lonely and it's a horrible feeling.

When you are sat on your stool after five very tough rounds and you've taken a lot of really hard punches and you still have seven rounds to go and you're thinking to yourself 'I can't go another seven rounds', that is the loneliest you will ever feel. Your trainer is telling you to do this and do that but he will be getting out the ring and going down the steps so his advice is going in one ear and out the other. There is someone at ringside who has probably never had a pair of boxing gloves on in his life and is screaming and shouting at you and you feel like jumping out the ring and smashing a couple of shots into his head. You are sat there feeling very low and that is the loneliest you will ever feel and that in my opinion is why boxing is the loneliest sport in the world. It is the greatest sport in the world and also the loneliest sport in the world.

I was now Commonwealth lightweight champion and was making the first defence of the title in my adopted hometown of Hartlepool. Also on the bill was the exciting Hartlepudlian and team mate of mine Michael Hunter, who was making his first defence of the British super-bantamweight crown against Marc Callahan. Hunter was unbeaten in 20 with a sole draw against Callahan and he wanted to put the record straight, so you can imagine there was a lot of needle in that fight. I'll tell you what, it didn't disappoint. It was non-stop action from the opening bell. What a fight. Hunter retained the title when the fight was stopped in the $10^{th}$ round but I'm getting ahead of myself here, so let's go back to my preparations for my first defence against 'Dynamite' Dean Philips from Wales.

It had been six months since my last fight against Jason Cook but I was looking forward to this one. I felt good and was confident and I had put the work in. After my 12 rounds for the IBO title I realised I could do the distance no problem, so the demons I had before had all disappeared. I didn't know much about Phillips other than he was super fit and he beat Michael Muya after me.

The sparring sessions I had in preparation were gruelling and my main sparring partner was a lad from Manchester called John Murray and we'd do 6 rounds, then 8 rounds, 10 and 12. We sparred a lot and every session was intense, you would pay money to watch those sparring sessions and go away with a smile on your face knowing you had definitely had your money's worth. John was an all-action fighter, he was non-stop and relentless. He had a great engine and would never let up with the volume of punches he threw, whether it was the first round or the $12^{th}$ round. Some days you would wake up and feel good and be up for the day's session and other days, especially when you were bringing your weight down to make weight, you wouldn't feel so good but you had John Murray coming for sparring so you knew you were in trouble. You had to be on your game with John. He was a proper workhorse and the sparring was second to none, but what a nice lad he was and we got on well. I said at the time he would win titles and I was proven right. He became British lightweight champion twice and European lightweight champion. He also fought for the World title in Madison Square Garden but just came up short.

Once the weigh-in was over I started to feel a bit nervous because the reality of defending the title in front of my home crowd was starting to kick in. Anyway once I was warmed up in the dressing room and ready to go the nerves had gone and had been taken over by adrenaline. I dropped Phillips in the second round and thought I was in for an early night, so I let the shots go but he took them well and stayed around so I stuck to my boxing and out-boxed him. Phillips was durable and had his little spells but I beat him comprehensively and found the 12 rounds no problem at all. The referee Phil Edwards scored the contest 118–111. The Commonwealth belt was placed around my waist and the ring announcer shouted: "And still Commonwealth lightweight champion, Kevin 'Bulldog' Bennett." I felt justified. Winning the title like I did didn't give me any satisfaction but this made up for it and I felt like a champion. It was a fantastic feeling successfully defending the title in front of a packed out Hartlepool Borough Hall. I took everything in and savoured the moment and what a special moment it was. The crowd were all on their feet cheering and clapping, it's something I'll never forget.

I was next booked to fight Graham Earl in a double title showdown. Earl's British title and my Commonwealth title were going to be on the line. Earl was unbeaten with a 22-0 log but instead of signing to fight me he wanted a 'warm up' fight first which delayed everything for about six months.

While this was going on and I was just ticking over, we got a call to see if I would go sparring in Denmark. I had no fights planned while I was waiting for Earl so I accepted. I flew from Newcastle and was met at Copenhagen airport, and then I was escorted to my palatial residence, a bed and breakfast above a pub.

I sparred every day for a week with the WBO Inter-Continental lightweight champion Martin Kristjansen, who was preparing for a European title fight. Most days we would do 8 rounds but we also did 10 rounds and a 12 rounder. He was a good boxer with decent skills but I was a bit too strong for him and had my own way and bossed the sparring. I damaged his nose in one of the spars and he had to wear a head guard with a bar across his face so as not to damage his nose any further. I enjoyed it out there and it was nice to get paid for sparring for a change.

Graham Earl had a 'warm up' fight and took on another unbeaten fighter called Ricky Burns in an eight rounder. I went down to the Wembley Conference Centre and watched it from ringside. Earl wasn't a fancy-dan with fast footwork, he was a plodder who came forward and wore opponents down so I couldn't believe they took Ricky Burns, whose style was all wrong for Earl. Burns was a mover and was slippy and sharp. He was a super-feather who moved like Willie Pep and Earl couldn't catch him. He out-sprinted Earl who should have taken another plodder as warm up. The Sky cameras came on me in a close up and I shook my head because I thought my fight with Earl had gone up in smoke. It was a close fight but Burns won it and I felt sick because I thought our fight was off, but once the dust settled I was told it was still on.

Once I was assured the Earl fight would be on I took a 'warm up' fight against a light-middleweight journeyman called Danny Moir. He was a big lad who towered over me but I used it as a work out and you know the old saying of kill the body and the head will fall, well that's what happened. Danny's punches were more of a thud and didn't feel like they had any snap in them. They would jar you but not hurt you. I used my small height to my advantage and got low and hit him to the body. He had to punch down and I was slipping his shots, so for the first two rounds I targeted his body and slipped in some rib ticklers and I could see I was breaking him down. I dropped him in the third round and they threw the towel in. Many years before this I sparred three rounds with him and he was a really nice lad, a gentleman, and I felt a bit bad for giving him a hammering.

I didn't really have a break I had a couple of days off and then it was full steam ahead for the double title showdown against Graham Earl. I was making the second defence of the Commonwealth strap and he was making the second defence of the British belt. The winner got both belts and won the bragging rights as the best lightweight in Great

Britain. I had a good camp and was as fit as a flea and had some great sparring with John Murray. He gave people nightmares with his pressure and he had a big heart to go with it. I always liked sparring with John he was an absolute warrior.

Everything was coming together at the right time and our camp was very confident we would win this fight. Not long before fight night we went down to London for a press conference because the fight was going to believe on Setanta pay per view. I remember saying to my coach Neil that Earl looked a bit on the heavy side. At the 11th hour, Earl pulled out and the fight got postponed and rescheduled three or four weeks later due to personal reasons for Earl. I was fuckin' fuming and sick as a chip, I had trained like a demon and was ready. The fight wasn't put back far enough so I could have time off so I carried on training. I think it was a tactic so I'd over-train. The camp seemed to go on forever and in my last spar against Murray I felt knackered. I wasn't far off the weight and didn't have the energy and felt weak and it was just over a week until the fight.

That summer night in the York Hall was unusually hot and humid and everyone was complaining about the heat and it just so happened that the air conditioning system was broken. The venue was full to the brim, so you can imagine the stifling heat and humidity of the place. It was the hottest venue I'd ever been in and it was draining the life out of me.

I was boxing well and winning the fight when I almost took his head off with a right hand. He got up and didn't know where he was, some referees would have stopped it there and then but the ref let it continue. I jumped on him and battered him all over the ring and he never threw another punch, he didn't know what day it was and was just trying to survive. I pummelled him in the corner and nothing was coming back and I was waiting for the ref to stop it. He was just about to jump in and stop the fight and crown me British champion, when he looked at Earl's corner, and Earl's manager who was also the show's promoter, shook his head to say 'don't stop it' and he didn't. That same referee has stopped lots of fights prematurely and for far less than this. That fight would have been stopped anywhere else. The bell ended the round and Earl survived. I had put a lot into that round trying to finish it so I started where I left off in the next round and tried to end it, he took more head shots but he hung in there and survived. My exertions caught up with me and I felt drained and the heat was really getting to me and draining the life out of me. Neil was telling me to keep Earl on the back foot, which I was doing, but by the end of the 8$^{th}$ round my fuel tank was running on empty. Earl had very good staying power and outlasted me. I was exhausted in the 9$^{th}$ and the fight was stopped, I hadn't been down, I hadn't been hurt, I was just depleted of energy and had nothing left. The heat beat me not Earl. I was gutted to lose that fight because I had it won. It was voted runner up in Great Britain's 'fight of the year' in 2005.

When I got home I went to my doctors and had some blood tests and they came back abnormal. They said my kidneys weren't functioning properly and weren't absorbing fluid. I think maybe I had flooded myself. If you couple that with the intense heat of the venue that night, it was a recipe for disaster. If I had the chance to do it all again, even in the baking conditions, I think it would have been a different result. I do think I fought the right fight and when I dropped him and proceeded to punch him from pillar to post, I do think the fight should have been stopped. If I had been in a bigger camp and the roles were reversed, the fight would have been stopped without a shadow of doubt. In my opinion it all boils down to politics and that was another example of it.

I knew after the fight that it was all over for me and I was retired. I had fought 47 championship rounds, not many people can say that. I got five grand for that fight and it was a double title fight between the number 1 and 2 in Great Britain, it was a piss take. It was a pittance and my manager didn't even take his cut because the money was so bad. I took Gemma to the Maldives with the money; we certainly deserved a holiday in paradise after all the years of blood, sweat and tears.

When we got back home all tanned and refreshed, I got a job working away for a cable firm and started earning some decent money. The phone rang and it was Denmark calling. They wanted me to go over for a few weeks sparring with the European champion Thomas Damgaard, who had a title fight coming up in America against Arturo Gatti. I was working away and had retired (though not officially) so I said thanks but no thanks.

I've also worked doing curtain walling and driving seven ton trucks but I went back to working on the cables around 12 years ago and I'm still doing it now for the same firm CBL Cable Contractors Ltd.

Although I retired from boxing I still liked to go to the gym and have a workout but now it was on my terms. I go to the gym when I want to and not because I had to like before. I have never been a big drinker and have never smoked. I don't do drugs and have never abused my body and like to think I'm still in pretty good shape. I was once asked how I would like the boxing world to remember me. Well I would like to be remembered for having a bit of everything. I could hit hard enough to get my opponents respect. I knocked a few out and I could take a punch, I only ever hit the canvas once in my full career amateur and professional. I could also box very well, so I would like to be remembered for having a bit of everything, on a smaller scale to my all-time favourite boxer Marvellous Marvin Hagler. Everyone has a favourite boxer and Marvin Hagler has always been mine, he had everything. He could box, he could fight, he could switch hit, he could take a punch and he had great stamina. He epitomizes the perfect all-round boxer for me. He was also a man of his word. When he said he was walking away from boxing after the Sugar Ray fight, he walked away and that was it. He achieved great things despite the odds being against him. He waited and waited for his chance and had over 40 fights before he got a title shot. He did it the hard way.

# ROUND 10

# PROFESSIONAL BOXING RECORD

## KEVIN BENNETT'S PROFESSIONAL BOXING RECORD

RECORD:

TOTAL FIGHTS 22

WON 17

LOST 5

## ABBREVIATION MEANINGS:

W = WON

L = LOST

KO = KNOCK OUT

TKO = TECHNICAL NOCK OUT

RTD = RETIRED ON STOOL

| DATE | OPPONENT | RESULT | VENUE |
|---|---|---|---|
| 01.12.99 | KARIM BOUALI | W PTS 4 | YARM |
| 28 MAR '00 | LES FROST | W TKO 2 | HARTLEPOOL |
| 25 JUN '00 | STEVE HANLEY | W PTS 6 | WAKEFIELD |
| 23 JUL '00 | GARY REID | W TKO 4 | HARTLEPOOL |
| 28 OCT '00 | GARY HARRISON | W RTD 2 | COVENTRY |
| 27 NOV '00 | TOMMY PEACOCK | W KO 5 | CRAWLEY |
| 3 MAR '01 | IAIN ELDRIDGE | W PTS 6 | WEMBLEY |
| 8 MAY '0 | KEITH JONES | W PTS 6 | HARTLEPOOL |
| 20 OCT '01 | PAUL DENTON | W PTS 6 | PORTSM'TH |
| 3 NOV '01 | MARK RAMSEY | W PTS 6 | GLASGOW |
| 26 JAN '02 | GLENN McCLARNON | L PTS 8 | DAGENHAM |
| 18 MAY '02 | COLIN LYNES | L TKO 4 | MILLWALL |
| 21 MAR '03 | KEITH JONES | W PTS 4 | WEST BROM |
| 21 JUN '03 | ZOLTAN SURMAN | W TKO 4 | MANC'R |
| 5 JUL '03 | COLIN DUNNE | W TKO 2 | BRENTWOOD |
| 8 NOV '03 | MICHAEL MUYA | W PTS 12 | WALE |
| | Commonwealth Lightweight Title | | |
| 1 MAY '04 | JASON COOK | L PTS 12 | WALES |
| | IBO World Lightweight Title | | |
| 19 NOV '04 | DEAN PHILLIPS | W PTS 12 | HARTLEPOOL |
| | Commonwealth Lightweight Title | | |
| 4 MAR '05 | DANNY MOIR | W TKO 3 | HARTLEPOOL |
| 19 JUN '05 | GRAHAM EARL | L TKO 9 | BETH' GREEN |
| | Commonwealth Lightweight Title & British Lightweight Title | | |

# PART THREE

# BARE KNUCKLE BOXING CHAMPION

# ROUND 11

# BARE KNUCKLE BOXER

Although I had retired from professional boxing and lived a normal life without boxing for the first time since I was nine, I enjoyed it. I was working away and earning good money and also became a father again in 2010. This time there wasn't just one but two, as Gemma gave birth to our twins, a boy and a girl we called Zack and Molly.

After ten years of being retired, I still felt I had a bit more left in me and I was back in the boxing ring but this time as a bare knuckle boxer. My pal was telling me about the bare knuckle boxing shows he had been going to and they sounded interesting and intriguing so I went along to the next show and really enjoyed it. I don't know what I was expecting to be honest, as I had only watched a few bare knuckle fights on the internet and I wasn't impressed and found them to be boring, maybe because they weren't fought in a ring and had too much room to move around.

I went to another show and enjoyed it as much as the first one. The fights were in a boxing ring with just a small bandage to protect the hands and everything else about it was just the same as going to a gloved boxing show. I was getting the buzz again, I could feel it and I knew I still had a few fights left in me. The promoters said they would love to have me on their shows so I had a think about it and decided to climb through the ropes once again. A few fights and it would be out of my system before father time came knocking, this was the last hurrah.

The next show was in Newcastle and I was matched with a 200 fight veteran called John Spencer. He had fought in all types of combat and I knew he was going to be game and tough. It was my first fight for ten years and my first BKB (Bare Knuckle Boxing) fight. I think all those years out had refreshed me because I was at my natural weight and I'd always kept myself fit I was just a lot older. I was hoping my boxing experience would make up for my age because it's a young man's game and I had fought at a level most people only dream about. I knew I had a better boxing brain and was confident of beating him.

After the weigh-in my coach Richy and I went to an Italian restaurant to get loaded up with pasta which became a ritual of ours. We spoke about concentrating on the body to save hand damage. We both knew that body punching was the key to bare knuckle boxing and I was always a good body puncher as a boxer, so I knew it would have more effect and hurt much more without the gloves. Funnily enough I wasn't that nervous it was a mixture of a small amount of nerves and excitement. A lot of supporters from Hartlepool came to watch including my former club mate Michael Hunter.

I walked to the ring with confidence, it was a week after my 40th birthday, and I had the fire back in my belly that hadn't been there for a while but felt like second nature, 'hello my old friend' I said silently. All my fans were singing and the atmosphere was red hot. The bell rang and I went straight on the attack, I wasn't going to mess about, I knew he was a good boxer and a bit clever during a few exchanges but I caught him with a good shot and after a delayed reaction the effects of it hit him and he took a knee. He got up and we engaged again and then I backed him up and a thunderous left hook to the body dropped him. A lot of men would have stayed down but this lad had balls and the fight continued but not for much longer. Another brutal body shot near the ropes dropped him and the fight was over in less than two minutes. There was still some fight and some bite left in The Bulldog.

I didn't fight again for a few months but kept ticking over in the gym with bag work and pad work and about four weeks out we'd step the training up with more intensity and Richy would put me through some intense pad sessions which got my fitness and conditioning spot on.

My next fight was in Nottingham against another 200 fight veteran called Mally Richardson and another good crowd of supporters came down to watch me and cheer me on. I have always been lucky that way, probably because I always gave value for money and my fans never went home disappointed. They weren't only 'fans' they were friends and family.

Richardson came straight at me throwing shots trying to surprise me but I walked through them and backed him up and he tripped in the ropes and fell down. He got up and the fight carried on as normal and he came at me throwing bombs, I slipped a few and he caught me with one, then I put him on the back foot and as soon as I sunk a body shot in, he went down grimacing in pain. He took a count but got back up and the ref waved it on and I went straight on the attack and hit him with four body punches, the last of which was a cracking left hook and he was back on the canvas. I didn't think he was getting back up but he made it and wanted more, this guy could take it. A few seconds later, after setting up a double left hook to the ribs, Richardson went down and out. It was all over in one minute and forty seconds.

Two fights, two wins, two first round knockouts and six knockdowns. Not bad if I do say so myself. The thing was I didn't really want any damage to myself like breaking a hand or any kind of injury like that because at my age, time wasn't on my side so a lengthy lay off to heal a broken bone was out of the question. We took it one fight at a time and it was going great so far. There were some final eliminators coming up at my weight for the World title and I was put forward to fight in them and got matched against the unbeaten Brad Harris.

I had seen Brad fight a couple of times and he had a nice boxing style but I'd had a long career as an amateur and pro and boxed at every level. If I hadn't seen your style I had seen something similar and always found a way past it. There wasn't anything you could show me that I hadn't already came across and that was my advantage and I was confident of victory.

A week before the fight I got some devastating news that took the wind out of my sails. My dog Hagler was crying all the time and obviously in pain, he was ok when he went for a walk but the other times he was whimpering and I knew something was up and phoned the vet. He was our baby, Gemma and I had him since before we had the kids. I explained the symptoms and the vet said it sounded like cancer and because of his age, if it was cancer, we might not be taking him back home.

He didn't have any obvious lumps anywhere but we still didn't hold out much hope as we made our way there. I walked him into the vets and had a guilty feeling like I was betraying him, it was terrible. I was hoping he would be alright but when the vet examined him she said Hagler had a cancerous tumour in his belly and because of his age, exploratory surgery would be unfair on him and the best thing to do for the dog was put him to sleep.

I was stroking him and cuddling him while the vet shaved a bit of his leg and put the needle in and he went to sleep in my arms. The vet left the room to give us some time with him and we cried our eyes out. During the drive home I had to pull over because I couldn't see through the tears. I've never felt pain like it and we as a family were grieving for our dog like we were grieving for a child. He was our child and a member of the family for 15 years.

We arranged for Hagler to be picked up and cremated and on the morning of my fight with Brad Harris, we got Hagler's ashes back and the grief hit us even harder, it was a double whammy. I felt weak and subdued all day and was in no frame of mind to fight but my experience in the fight game told me to get on with it.

Richy didn't say much on the way to Coventry, he knew I was in no mood to laugh and joke about anything so he kept the conversations brief, he knows me personally and has had his own fair share of grief so he knew what I was going through. Fighting was the last thing on my mind but that's why we were in Coventry and we had a job to do.

After the weigh-in, we went for some pasta and chilled out for a bit before heading to the arena. As the night drew on the fight was almost upon us and I got ready into my fight gear and Richy was geeing me up and trying to get my mind in fight mode, he said the right things at the right time. In the ring I knew I had to go about business. Brad was a good and capable lad and I knew I had to get on top of him. He was one of them boxers that if you stand off and let him do his stuff, he was very dangerous. The bell rang and I closed him down and didn't give him any room. It was an entertaining first round with some quality boxing on display, I sunk a couple of body shots into him but he took them well. The second round was more of the same and I hit him with some decent body shots and in an act of defiance or bravado, he waved me in 'come on'. I knew they were hurting him and he couldn't take too many before they caught up with him. Near the end of the round I landed a straight right hand flush on the jaw and Brad was on the deck. He got up and the bell rang to end the round and I had to wait another minute to press my advantage. I think that's when the doubts set in to Brad's mind and he realised he was going to be on the wrong end of it. Coming out for the third I wanted to get on him and finish it. He had a go and showed heart and grit but I dropped him again with a right hand over the top. He got back up after taking a count and the fight continued. He had so far taken some good wallops to the body and taken them well, but I got him on the ropes and dropped him for the third time with a vicious hook to the body. He got up and the fight was almost over when I buckled his legs with a body shot and the bell rang to end the fight and I won a unanimous decision.

He came to see me in the dressing room and showed me all the red and purple welts all over his body and was in a bit of pain. He limped out of the dressing room and I knew he would be sore for a few days or more. He was a brave lad.

Sean George won the other final eliminator and he would be the one I was to fight for the World title in a few months. He got in the ring and we did a 'face off' for the cameras.

# ROUND 12

# WORLD TITLE

The date was set for my World title fight, August 13 at the Colwick Hall Hotel in Nottingham, two days before my 41st birthday. It was over five rounds as that is the title fight distance in BKB. It would be a history making fight if I won because I would be the first person ever to be an amateur boxing champion, a professional boxing champion and a bare knuckle boxing champion. We discussed it and agreed it would be a unique treble. Although I hadn't heard of anyone claiming to have won all three in the past, no doubt someone might have 'claimed' the treble but anyone can do that. I would be the first to do it 'officially' and all my title wins come with certificates, trophies, belts, programmes, documentation and videos of proof.

When I set out on this bare knuckle journey with Richy, we said we would take it one fight at a time and barring injuries or defeat, see how far we can go. I still had the fire in my belly and wanted this title which was for the WBKBC (World Bare Knuckle Boxing Council) belt.

A little bit about my opponent Sean George, a hard as nails Welshman from the valleys. His grandfather had been a professional boxer so fighting was in his blood, and as a teenager Sean became interested in all forms of fighting and learned lots of different styles, Muay Thai, Jiu Jitsu, Kick Boxing and MMA.

"I loved the thrill and buzz of full contact" he said, "In the gym sparring, whether I was getting beat on or beating on someone else, I always walked out of the gym feeling good."

He started to train hard and built his fitness levels up because he knew fitness was a 'key factor'. He fought for his country wearing the Welsh Dragon with pride in full contact kick boxing fights. He also became British champion at Muay Thai and won an MMA title. Bare knuckle was like second nature to him and he knew he 'had the tools' to be very good at it. I also knew that I had to be in great shape because this lad would bring some thunder.

Luckily for me I was working local and was able to put plenty of gym work in. We done some training at the beach which I enjoyed and the intense pad work was getting me fit and fast, I was sharp as a tack and felt really strong. I was as ready as I'd ever be.

A couple of weeks before the fight, Richy phoned me and told me about a dream he had. He said he was browsing in a shop and he came across two Marvin Hagler mugs that were in a glass case, both were totally different and he knew he had to buy them both because 'two' would be important. He opened the case and took them out and went to the counter where an old woman with silver/grey hair served him. When he walked out the shop he got the feeling he had to buy the two mugs because they represented two titles and I would win two championship belts. We didn't realise how significant that 'dream' was until after I retired. Marvin Hagler is also my favourite boxer. He said we should wear Marvin Hagler t-shirts for the title fight because it's an omen. If you watch the video you will see us with our Hagler t-shirts on. I never really thought much about it because Richy has said stuff to me in the past that has made my hairs stand on end and I know he tells the truth. He is a straight talker and doesn't tell fairy tales, he isn't that kind of man.

It was a great vibe travelling down to Nottingham, we had an Elvis CD blasting out all the King's greatest hits and we were singing our heads off. The mood was good and the confidence was high.

After the weigh-in when we faced off, Sean was a lot taller than me and one of his supporters shouted 'Easy work Sean' and I remember us saying to each other after it 'We'll fuckin' see'. The tickets for this fight sold out as soon as they went on sale and coaches, vans and cars made their way to the venue from all over the country. Sean brought lots of fans from Wales and I had loads from Hartlepool as well as my parents and some family who made the trip from the Black Country. The atmosphere was electric. You see at the bare knuckle boxing shows there is never any trouble, all the fighting is done in the ring.

Everything we had done in preparation had led to this moment. Everything was ready. I was ready, fighting togs on, small length of bandage wrapped and taped on each hand, warmed up and waiting for the call to make my entrance. The tension, the excitement, the adrenaline, the anticipation and the buzz from the crowd, all rolled into one. It's hard to put it into words to do it justice but it's an experience you will never forget. Everything I've just mentioned went up another level when my name was announced and my music came on (We Will Rock You by Queen) and I made my way to the ring.

Sean was tall and a bit rangy, we had watched him and most of his work was long distance. He had a good jab and some great straight shots. His jab was his main weapon and he used it to set his other shots up. We knew he had power because we had seen him drop a few people. We worked on a game plan to take his jab away and counter it and stop him throwing it, get low and work the body and keep switching the attacks and keep working. I hurt him with a body shot in the first round and his elbow came down and also gave him a small cut to the side of his left eye. I was mixing it up so he didn't know where the attack was coming from and everything he threw I countered it, so subsequently he stopped throwing as much and I had him on the back foot. I cut the ring off and made him work hard and he was back-peddling faster than he wanted. I was dictating the pace but he was game as a badger.

In the second round I caught him with a sweet shot under the eye and when it landed it made a loud crack and his cheek bone started to swell immediately. The third round was more of the same, a blistering pace and I doubled up on the jab. He caught me round with back of the head with a right hand and I stumbled into the corner post but I was off it in a flash. I rocked his head back with a sold jab and his right eye was bleeding. I can remember at the end of the third round his eye was almost closed and the ref went over to his corner and Sean was shaking his head because he didn't want the fight to be stopped. There was no quit in him he was as brave as they come.

At the end of the rounds the announcer would ask people to sit down to stop blocking other people's views because the fight was so exciting they couldn't help but jump up and roar us both on. I caught Sean with some sickening shots which knocked his head back and he took them and fought back, what a warrior. I didn't have it all my own way because he made a great fight of it.

After four rounds of that we still had one to go and coming out for the last round Richy told me to relax and take my time and don't do anything stupid, but everybody had witnessed four rounds of war and I wanted to close the show in style, so did Sean, and we went toe-to-toe with the crowd on their feet going mental. I trapped him in his own corner and hit him with a flurry of shots and he was throwing back and the crowd were going wild. During a brief second of breath I clapped my hands together to say 'let's have it' and he obliged until the bell ended it. Everyone knew they had just witnessed something special and people were saying it was the best fight they'd ever seen. I think I won every round with the closest being the last round when we both threw caution to the wind. Sean was physically exhausted and if he hadn't been so fit he wouldn't have made it, nobody else would have taken that amount of punishment. After the final bell I knew I'd won it and after the hugs and pleasantries came the announcement:

"The Winner by unanimous decision, and the new, World lightweight bare knuckle champion, Kevin 'Bulldog' Bennett."

All my supporters were singing 'There's only one Kevin Bennett' and I did a quick interview in the ring and said I knew Sean was going to be tough but didn't realise he would be that tough. I thanked my supporters and Sean's supporters and everyone cheered and appreciated that.

The adrenaline and the buzz afterwards was unbelievable, I had done the treble and made history as the only man 'officially' to be an Amateur boxing champion, Professional boxing champion and Bare knuckle boxing champion.

In the dressing room afterwards, Sean was being sick and went to hospital for a check-up. He had a fractured cheek bone, a broken nose and concussion.

My hands came up like puddings and I could hardly lift a cup, it was testament to how tough Sean George was and how much punishment he withstood. He was a pure warrior and I have nothing but praise and respect for him. We became good friends. He is humble and respectful, a great bloke and a gentleman, hats off to Sean George.

As a postscript to this a lot of people on social media were praising Sean for his bravery and rightly so but nobody hardly mentioned me, you would think Sean won. I never got any praise off the promoters, not even a hand shake or a well done and I found it very strange.

Sean had lost a very close decision to Brad Harris in his third fight, a decision that could have gone either way. I beat Brad convincingly and I was unbeaten and thought I deserved to be favourite; but I still went to the ring first and never made a big deal out of it. Sean's mother even noticed and wrote a statement on social media saying, "Let us praise Kevin Bennett, let's not forget he won a World title. He took time out during his victory, when he should have been celebrating with his family and friends. He came up to Sean in the dressing room and put his arm around him to make sure he was alright and he also consoled me."

It was great to win the title and do it so convincingly. We were gentlemanly and gracious about it which is the way it should be.

A few days later when I sat down with Richy he said "We did what we set out to do, stayed undefeated and won the World title, now let's retire at the top."

I said no because I wanted to make the belt my own and to do that I had to make three defences. "Are you sure you don't want to retire" he said. "Three more fights and I'm done," I said, "it'll be all over."

My first World title defence was at the Lancastrian Suite in Gateshead on Bonfire night. My original opponent Nathan Leeson pulled out two weeks before fight night with a shoulder injury. I was disappointed because I really fancied that one, but my old foe Brad Harris stepped up to the mark and took the job as he was already in training for another fight. We were confident of victory because I hadn't beaten him when I wasn't at my best (my mind was elsewhere after losing my dog) and I was sure there would be only one result and that was another win for me. I was working in Scotland and it was hard to find a gym where we lodged so after work I'd go running and shadow box and do other exercises. I was home at weekends and every Saturday and Sunday Richy would give me some intense pad work in the gym followed by the medicine ball. I was fit and strong and in a good frame of mind.

On the morning of the fight, The Dark Destroyer Nigel Benn was in Hartlepool so before we headed off to Gateshead for the weigh-in, we went to see him and had a chat and a photo with him and his parting words were "Good luck in tonight's fight."

What a good venue the Lancastrian Suite was, we were all happy with it when we had a look around the place. After the weigh-in we went to the Metro Centre to an Italian restaurant and got some fuel down us in the shape of a plate of pasta which was our usual pre-fight meal. Richy's wife Wendy and her friend Rachel was with us and also Dean Kitching, who was going to do some photography at the show. He was mainly there to photograph my fight but he said he would snap away at most of the bouts. Incidentally Dean took some incredible pictures of all the fights. After our meal I went to my hotel for a lay down and chill out, there was no need for me to get there early because I was on last so I arrived half way through the show. I went upstairs to the dressing room and Richy said "I'll show you were your fans are." And we headed to a balcony that overlooked the show, what a great spot it was and who was there clicking away with his camera, our mate

Dean and he'd already got some great shots. I looked over the balcony and one of the lads spotted me and pointed up and within seconds hundreds of people were singing 'There's only one Kevin Bennett' it's something I'll never forget and I got goose bumps. There was a fight going on in the ring at the time.

I remember Ray Cann was handing up for us for the first time that night and he was nervous and couldn't sit down and I was calming him down. I said "Ray there's nothing to be nervous about. You don't have to pass a stool up because I don't sit down. Richy will ask you for water, spit-bucket, ice bag, just pass him them and don't worry." He replied "I can't believe you are so calm." We were always calm. We were always chilled until it was time to get ready for action and get warmed up and into fight mode. Ray was a talented amateur boxer who fought the likes of Joe Calzaghe and Paul Ingle but the reason he stopped was because he used to get so nervous before fights.

I got warmed up and we were ready to go, the atmosphere was brilliant and I got a buzz off the crowd. I had been going on the sunbed in Scotland to get myself nice and tanned as I didn't want to look like a milk bottle in the ring, but I overdone it and burnt myself. I was thinking I hope he doesn't hit me in the body because it will sting like fuck.

I went on the attack from the get go and the first round was exciting with some pretty good boxing on display, then near the end of the round, he tried to slip a shot but I caught him with an overhand right that seemed to cuff him at the side of the ear but more towards the back of the head and he went down in the corner. GGG throws similar shots to the one I landed and look what happens to his opponents. He beat the count but I think the knock down took a bit out of him and put him in survival mode and the writing was on the wall from then on. He done a lot of complaining about different things and it was a case of when and not if. He did give me a little nick over the eye in the second round when he landed a flurry but it was more out of desperation and that was his only success. I dropped him a couple of times in the second round. He complained about his back, his hand, his hip, but I just stayed on him and after going down another twice in the third round, he got up and walked over to me and shook my hand and the fight was all over. That was another win in the bag, two more successful defences and then retirement.

# ROUND 13

# GOING OUT AT THE TOP

The promoters were putting a show on the week before Christmas in Hartlepool and there was going to be awards handed out and a full bill of bare knuckle fights. It was the first BKB show ever to be held in Hartlepool and they asked me if I would defend my title and be top of the bill. I needed time to think because I fought on Nov 5 and didn't want to be back in the ring so soon because my hands were usually very painful for two or three weeks after a fight. Anyway call me crazy but after thinking about it I said yes because I wanted to be a part of history in the town and I would be top of the bill, the champ defending the title in his home town. What could go wrong!

I was making the second defence of my title and was working away and could only get to the gym when I was home at weekends. I was supposed to be fighting Nathan Leeson who pulled out last time, but he said he wasn't ready for some reason or other, so we had to get another opponent and we said we'd fight anyone and the name Liam James came to the forefront. He had an MMA background and was Conor McGregor's sparring partner. Everyone wanted to be at this show and I sold a shed load of tickets.

On the day of the show the local council said the show had to be moved and couldn't be held at the venue because it didn't hold a drinks license (the main venue had already been booked for a Christmas party by the local Rigby club) and it was too close to a built up area and would be a noise nuisance, so rather than cancelling the show, the promoters moved it over the road to a venue that was totally inadequate and had no heating. It was so cold it was like holding a show outside in the North Pole, it was horrendous. Lots of people walked out and left because they were so cold. It was the worst show I had ever been to, it was a total farce and I should have known that something untoward was in the frozen air.

My opponent had his bandages signed off by the WBKBC official Sammy Morris and unknown to us at the time, Liam James took them bandages off, for whatever reason only he knows, and replaced them with his own wraps and own tape both of which had been banned by the WBKBC. Nothing was said and no action was taken before, during or after about it. How incompetent is that. What a joke.

We had seen Liam and knew what to expect, he comes out the traps a million miles an hour and then blows a gasket; but because of his MMA background he liked to pull your head down. I wouldn't have expected him to come in and box but at the same time I wouldn't have expected him to get away with what he got away with.

The first round he came out the traps a million miles an hour as expected and threw a few shots, nothing significant, then he pulled my head down and hit me with three or four uppercuts while pulling my head down onto his punches. He then pulled me off balance by the back of the head, I steadied myself ready to go in and the referee called time and took me to see the doctor and at this stage I didn't know why as I didn't know I was cut. When the referee calls time the timekeeper stops the clock and the fight wasn't 20 seconds old. The doctor said the cut was very nasty and to the bone and he couldn't let me continue. I protested and wanted to carry on, even just given a chance to see the round out but the doctor said no, the injury was too bad. The cut was unlike anything I or anyone else had ever seen and we'd been in the fight game a lot of years. It was a puncture wound and looked like I'd been hit with a sharp object and not a fist with a bandage on it. Liam said he broke his hand in four places and if that was true he wouldn't have made it past the first round.

We knew the rules of boxing and expected it to be declared a no-contest and it wasn't, they awarded the fight to Liam and gave him the belt and everyone started booing.

The rules from the British Boxing Board of Control say:

Doctor's Stoppage/Injury: The fighter has suffered and cannot continue the match safely.

In some cases, an accidental injury (such as a clash of heads), once a match becomes official (more than half the distance or four rounds in most jurisdictions) is grounds for the fight being declared finished and a valid decision is made.

In layman's terms if the doctor stops the fight through injury and the fight is less than half way through or less than four rounds, it is declared a no-contest.

This was an injury caused by holding my head down and punching it, illegal in boxing. The fight was less than twenty seconds old when the Doctor was called and wasn't going long enough for it to be declared official. It would be different if it was a knock out but it was a Doctor's stoppage through injury less than twenty seconds into the fight. Anyone with half a brain knows it's a no-contest. It was a farce.

By the time Liam's hand healed and the bullet hole in my forehead had healed, four months had passed. It was along four months and it felt like going through a long winter waiting for spring. The rematch was set for April 23 in Coventry.

During that time there was a lot of arguments between my fans and Liam's on social media and I only ever wrote one thing and that was when Liam was getting lippy and disrespectful. My mother wrote something saying to Liam that he should conduct himself more gentlemanly and he responded with something ungentlemanly. This guy had no manners.

I wasn't into the Facebook arguments, you don't win fights on Facebook but I posted a reply to Liam and said:

"You are confident in your ability and I am confident in mine, so why don't we have a winner takes all. The winner gets both purses and the loser gets nothing. I'm willing to put my confidence in my ability are you willing to do the same?"

He never answered for a while and people kept asking him for an answer so eventually he said something like 'I don't want to take the food out of his mouth, I've got what I want' or words to that effect. I wasn't expecting that and it's not a reply that someone confident in his own ability would write. That told me all I needed to know and gave me the advantage. I already knew I was the better boxer and there was no way he could beat me other than a freak 'accident'. When he never accepted the challenge of 'winner takes all', I knew that he knew he wasn't the better man, so psychologically I had him beat. If he had accepted the challenge and thought in his own mind that he could win, I knew he would have been still half in it, but when he answered like he did, I knew the psychological battle was won.

A stroke of luck was when I was put on a local job and I knew I could have a good training camp and be fully prepared. I hadn't worked local since I was training for the Sean George fight so that was the last good training camp I had. The other times I had to do my own thing during the week and get my gym work in on weekends when I was home. The omens were looking good and the positive vibe only got stronger.

I had wanted to retire in December after that shambolic decision left everyone scratching their heads in disbelief, but because Liam James had made it personal and had been disrespectful on social media, I felt like I had to prove a point otherwise I would have retired.

We had a great training camp and everyone wanted to help in any way they could. We brought in Steven Smith as a strength and conditioning coach because that was his thing and he was very good at it so I worked with him a couple of times a week.

Richy was putting me through some pads on the beach in the fresh air when all of a sudden the heavens opened, Ste Cotson's gym was round the corner and he welcomed us in and let us train free of charge. We went sparring every Tuesday to another gym and I did six hard rounds for six weeks with the talented Luke Cope. Our tactics were for me to box on the back foot, slip and counter and for Luke to come forward throwing shots non-stop, pressure, pressure, pressure. We both boxed out of our comfort zone but it worked a treat.

The game-plan was to box on the back foot, with lots of head movement and slipping and to make him miss and punish him with counters, and as Richy said to me a few times: "Skill, Brains and Guts will win this fight."

We knew Liam would be good for two rounds and then blow a gasket. We never questioned his desire to win and always knew he was tough and game.

We spoke in training about how we thought the fight would go and I said "He'll be made to miss, he'll get frustrated, he'll be getting out-boxed and getting hurt and he'll either quit with an injury or I'll stop him." That was what I said from day one. I sold another shed load of tickets for this one, every man and his dog wanted to be at this fight. Even people who had nothing to do with boxing were sending messages wanting to see him beaten because of the way he conducted himself.

We shared a changing room with the American fighters Shonie Carter and Melvin Guillard. We all just talked and chilled out and it was really laid back. It was super chilled but when it was getting near fight time each fighter would change into their war clothes and warm-up; then would be called to the ring and walk out to the gladiatorial arena. It was another day at the office but our office involved blood and pain.

I was warmed up and waiting in the wings ready to be called to the ring, this time as the challenger, when my music came on and we were off. We had waited four months for this and it was finally here and lots of people were shouting well wishes from everywhere in the arena.

Liam came out the blocks as expected, like the Tasmanian devil. I came underneath him and threw a right hook over the top and cut him straight away with more or less one of the first shots of the fight. He came again and left his feet behind and I moved to the side and pulled him out the way and he fell over. I was making him miss a lot; he had a bit of success but not much worth shouting about. He was calling me towards him and I knew he was frustrated and we were only a minute into the fight. He couldn't cope with my ability to slip shots but that's how we planned it and everything was going to plan. He was putting everything he had into his punches and by the second round he was breathing heavy, being made to miss was catching up with him and he was running out of steam. When I got back to my corner after the second round Richy said: "He's finished, he's got nothing left. Go out this round and knock him out."

I was getting Vaseline on my face when I noticed some commotion in his corner and the referee waving it off signalling the fight was over. I said 'the fight's been stopped'

Richy was facing me with his back to their corner and turned around and looked and gave out a loud 'Yesss' and you could hear four months of frustration in that yell. Liam didn't go out on his shield. He quit. He knows deep down that if he didn't quit he would have got knocked out. Then all the excuses came out and he said he broke his hand. He lost fair and square but he didn't lose with dignity.

I had regained my title that I should never have lost and was now a two-time World champ. They had just got rid of the old belts and issued new ones and I was presented with the new one which I was allowed to keep because in reality it was my third defence and I deserved it.

Thinking back now, remember that dream Richy had before the Sean George fight that I would win two belts? Well I did win two belts. Maybe it was a premonition.

I had beaten everyone who was around at the time in my weight division and it was now time to say goodbye. Five days later I put a notice on social media to say I had retired. Here it is:

"I'm not into writing statuses but here goes. Many of you have been good to me and I feel it's only right, and polite, to say that it is all over. I started this journey in August 2015 a week after my 40th birthday. Richy and I spoke about giving the BKB a go and said we would win what was on offer. Obviously things took off and challenges were presented. I feel we rose to them challenges and gave our all achieving what we set our minds to, but like all good things, there comes a time to walk away.

I will be 42 in August and I juggle a full-time job that takes me the length and breadth of the country, and abroad at times, I also have a family, four children to be precise and they need my time. You can imagine setting time aside for training, and getting rest isn't easy and father time is knocking at my door.

Anyway I've rambled on enough, so a massive thank you to all the fans out there what have supported me and especially those who have travelled the length and breadth of the country to be at my fights.

I wouldn't be right if I didn't say a massive thank you to my coach and more importantly my friend Richy, who has put as much time into this as I have and for very few plaudits, so thanks mate. I couldn't and wouldn't have done it with anyone else."

To my surprise I got a letter of congratulations off the notorious prisoner Charles Bronson, who had changed his name to Charles Salvador. It said:

"Kevin,

*WOW,*

*What a fucking roller coaster ride you had with Richy,*

*Amazing,*

*And retired at the TOP,*

*I can only salute you,*

*MAX RESPECT,*

*Charles Salvador AKA Bronson*

In December 2017 in a poll on the internet, the fans voted that I was the best pound for pound British BKB fighter ever and if that wasn't enough my fight with Sean George was voted as the best BKB fight ever.

In January 2018 I was invited to the Mayor of Hartlepool's chamber to receive an award for 'Outstanding Achievement in Sport' for my services and accomplishments in the fight game.

I still go to the local amateur gym and help train the next crop of young champions. It's nice to give a bit back.

That was my journey and I hope you enjoyed 15 rounds with the Bulldog.

Don't forget to read all the tributes and memories in round 15 which is the final chapter. I'm sure you will enjoy them because they have been an important part of my journey of being, 30 Years A Fighter.

Thank You

Kevin 'Bulldog' Bennett

# ROUND 14

# BARE KNUCKLE BOXING RECORD

| DATE | OPPONENT | RESULT | VENUE |
|---|---|---|---|
| 22 AUG '15 | JOHN SPENCER | W TKO1 | NEWCASTLE |
| 7 NOV '15 | MALLY RICHARDSON | W TKO 1 | NOTTINGHAM |
| 7 MAY '16 | BRAD HARRIS | W PTS 3 | COVENTRY |

Title eliminator

| 13 AUG '16 | SEAN GEORGE | W PTS 5 | NOTTINGHAM |
|---|---|---|---|

World Lightweight Bare Knuckle Boxing Title

| 5 NOV '16 | BRAD HARRIS | W TKO 3 | GATESHEAD |
|---|---|---|---|

World Lightweight Bare Knuckle Boxing Title

| 17 DEC '16 | LIAM JAMES | L RTD 1 | HARTLEPOOL |
|---|---|---|---|

World Lightweight Bare Knuckle Boxing Title

Bennett lost title on a cut when fight was stopped after 20 seconds by the Doctor. The rules state that it should be ruled a no-contest.

| 23 APR '17 | LIAM JAMES | W RTD 2 | COVENTRY |
|---|---|---|---|

World Lightweight Bare Knuckle Title

Regained World Lightweight Bare Knuckle Title

28 APR '17 RETIRED AS CHAMPION

# TRIBUTES AND MEMORIES

# CHRIS BESSEY MBE

## ABA WELTERWEIGHT CHAMPION 1993

## 5 X ABA LIGHT-MIDDLEWEIGHT CHAMPION 1995, 97, 98, 99, 00.

## GOLD MEDAL COMMONWEALTH GAMES LIGHT-MIDDLEWEIGHT 1998

I sparred with Benny a few times in the Army. I was a stone and a half heavier than him and a few inches taller and maybe had a four inch longer reach. He always said I had long arms but I just extended my reach and pivoted more. He was a body snatcher and it could take a lot out of you if you got hit with them. I tended not to get hit with them but when he got inside he worked well and was a real pain in the arse. He'd hit you in the body and switch it over the top. His style was suited much more to the pro game. He had a good record but he was so much better than his record suggests, he was a quality fighter.

# COLIN 'DYNAMO' DUNNE

## WBU WORLD LIGHTWEIGHT CHAMPION

I was WBU World champ for five years and had 38 wins in 40 fights when I fought Kevin Bennett in my last fight, it wasn't supposed to be my last fight but that is how it turned out.

I used to roll a lot it was my style, up and down, roll, roll, roll and he hit me on top of the head with a short chopping right. It sent an electrical jolt through my body and my legs went. The ref gave me a count and I got up and he waved the fight to continue and fair play to Kev he just went in for the kill, like you would.

He hit me with a left hook at the back of the jaw and I was on the canvas again. My arms and legs were moving like I was doing an Elvis Presley impression and the ref waved it off. There was no way I could have continued.

That was the first time anything like that had ever happened to me and Kevin spoke very highly of me afterwards.

Last year I was walking around the Olympic Stadium when I heard someone shout 'Colin Dunne', I had a quick look round and couldn't see anyone so continued walking and heard it again 'Colin Dunne'. I turn around and see about five lads sat there and I didn't recognise any of them until one stood up and took his sunglasses off and it was Kevin Bennett.

I said: "You caught me with a lucky punch that night. It was lucky for you and unlucky for me" and we had a good chat. What a nice bloke he was.

# DEREK ROCHE

## BRITISH WELTERWEIGHT CHAMPION

I had lost the British Welterweight title and my unbeaten record a few months previous and was preparing for a comeback fight when Kevin came through for some sparring. He was only a two or three fight pro novice so I was expecting it to be nice and steady but he gave me a shock, he was like a little ball of fire. He was very sharp and had plenty of guts and just kept coming at me, it was good for me because it kept me on my toes. When you are young and coming through, sometimes you feel like you have something to prove and have to stand your ground and make your mark and that's what he did. He gained my respect straight away. I knew he was going to get somewhere and I was right.

# WAYNE ALEXANDER

## ABA LIGHT-MIDDLEWEIGHT CHAMPION 1994

## WBU WORLD LIGHT-MIDDLEWEIGHT CHAMPION

## BRITISH LIGHT-MIDDLEWEIGHT CHAMPION

I remember Kevin from when he was an amateur he was always in the Army team when they fought London and I was in the London team. He was top drawer. I remember he was very tough and durable with a come forward style as an amateur and he carried that into the pro game. I hadn't seen him for about ten years and bumped into him at a function night for a boxer it was good to catch up.

I watched some of his fights on Sky and he could take a good shot as well as give one. I respected his heart and desire and I've watched some of his bare knuckle fights on the internet. He is one hard man.

# ARV MITTOO

## ABA NOVICE CHAMPION

## 100 PRO FIGHTS AT WELTERWEIGHT

I sparred with Kevin once and I couldn't lay a glove on him, the man was pure class and boxed the head off me.

Afterwards I was thinking I wished I could be half as good as him, he was really skilled. It was that spar that inspired me to be the best that I could and I went on to have 100 professional fights.

Kevin Bennett was an animal in the ring and a gentleman outside it.

# JASON COOK

ABA FEATHERWEIGHT CHAMPION 1993

COMMONWEALTH GAMES SILVER MEDAL 1994

EUROPEAN LIGHTWEIGHT CHAMPION

IBO WORLD LIGHTWEIGHT CHAMPION

I fought Kevin twice; the first time was in the quarter-finals of the national schoolboy championships. He was a come forward fighter and so was I and we slugged it out for three rounds in a thriller. It was a really tough fight.

Our second fight was when I defended the IBO World title against him and everyone was expecting fireworks and got the opposite. We showed each other too much respect and it was a dull 12 rounds.

Kevin was a hell of a fighter and should have achieved more. I feel he under achieved but I think it was because he fought most of his career in a heavier weight division and should have been a lightweight from the start. I was a big lightweight so I was fighting a weight below myself, but it was the opposite way for Kevin, he was fighting a weight above himself. Winning the Commonwealth title was a great achievement in itself. Well done Kevin.

# MICHAEL HUNTER

ABA FLYWEIGHT CHAMPION 1997

ABA BANTAMWEIGHT CHAMPION 1999

NABC CHAMPION 1997

WBF SUPER BANTAMWEIGHT CHAMPRION

BRITISH, COMMONWEALTH & EUROPEAN SUPER BANTAMWEIGHT CHAMPION

IBF SUPER BANTAMWEIGHT TITLE CHALLENGER

There were four of us at the Hartlepool Boys Welfare who were open class boxers, Benny and me, Ian Cooper and Billy Bessey. The phone would ring and that would be it. Let's get it on!

We would jump in the mini-bus and travel the length and breadth of the country fighting anyone, anywhere, they were great days.

Benny had long arms for a short lad so it was deceiving how good his reach was. I had a straight nose until I sparred with him BANG. I knew it was broke before it was confirmed to be. He had a lot of power and was a very hard man. He had the potential to be world champion at lightweight or light-welterweight. What a great fighter.

# JOHN MURRAY

## 2 X BRITISH LIGHTWEIGHT CHAMPION

## EUROPEAN LIGHTWEIGHT CHAMPION

## WBA LIGHTWEIGHT TITLE CHALLENGER

I had some very good sparring sessions with Kevin; they were intense and were a very important part of my education that led to my successful career. Kevin was a strong lad and a good inside fighter. I remember learning a lot from my sparring sessions with him.

# JOHN PEARCE

2 X ABA MIDDLEWEIGHT CHAMPION 1996 & 98

NABC CHAMPION CLASS A

MULTI-NATIONS SILVER MEDAL 1996

BLACK SEA CUP SILVER MEDAL UKRAINE 1997

MULTI-NATIONS GOLD MEDAL 1998

COMMONWEALTH GAMES GOLD MEDAL 1998

I remember one Sunday morning at the England training camp in Crystal Palace. I didn't sleep well and was up early and I'm looking out the window in the big tall tower, it was a bit misty and hazy and I thought I saw a taxi pull up which I thought was a bit strange. Then I saw three lads get out and as they got closer it was Benny, Chris and Paul. I looked at my watch and we were about 50 minutes away from getting up for our morning run. They came walking in steaming and I was stood there giggling at them and Chris came in and absolutely hummed of drink. I went over to Benny and said "I've just seen you three come in." His reply was "I'm dreading this run." I was thinking 'yes I'll be able to beat Chris here' but believe me I just managed to keep up with him.

I always remember Benny was out drinking a lot on the England team but he was a squaddie and they all love a drink. He was easily led or so he says.

I remember when the England team sparred and it didn't matter who was in the ring, whenever someone got caught and their head snapped back, Benny would shout 'Bungeeeee', it was quite funny.

At the draw for the Multi-Nations we were sat there and Benny was telling us "If you get drawn against an itchy-cough, scratchy-cough or any other cough it is plan B."

We were a bit naive and Benny said "Have you packed for plan B?"

I said to him "What's plan B?" He laughed and said "plan B is if you go out in the first round then you are on the drink for the next week and need your dancing shoes, that's plan B, any type of cough is plan B. Itchy or scratchy that means a Russian, Ukrainian or Eastern European." He was laughing as we were sat there waiting for the draw having a bit craic and he got drawn with a cough and he said "Fuckin' hell it looks like plan B after today." He had us all laughing our heads off. Benny and Micky Thompson both went out in the first round and Micky hadn't packed anything for plan B and the doormen wouldn't let him in the club in his trainers so Benny lent him a pair of shoes. Micky is a ten and Benny is an eight but he wore them for four days on the lash, his feet were knackered and he could hardly walk at the end of it.

Benny was a proper lad who I gelled with from day one. He was as rough as Bulls lugs, a proper fighter. He could have a real tear up but he was clever. He never got an easy draw he always got the top lads in the World.

All the top Eastern Europeans who Benny always got drawn against had to be at the top of their game to keep him in check and they had to raise their game even higher to beat him. They start off as they need to and have a little look and see how you are and do just enough to get through, but they always had to do more than enough to beat Benny. He was a great fighter.

# YOUNG MUTLEY

## BRITISH WELTERWEIGHT CHAMPION

I remember fighting Kevin in the amateurs and he won the decision. I didn't forget it when I was asked to go and spar with him and thought to myself 'yes, I can get my own back'. I was British Welterweight Champion at the time.

I was hitting him with lots of jabs and combinations as he constantly came forward. I can't remember the punch exactly but I think it was a screw left uppercut that I caught him with and broke his nose. There was lots of blood and his nose wouldn't stop bleeding. He was very game and tough.

# NIGEL WRIGHT

## 2 X ABA LIGHT-WELTERWEIGHT CHAMPION 1998 & 00

## MULTI-NATIONS SILVER MEDAL 1999

Mine and Benny's rivalry turned out to be huge and started in 1998 in the quarter finals of the ABAs. It was my first attempt at the ABAs and Benny was established on the England team. He had big muscles and a few tattoos and he looked mean. I never feared anyone but this was the first time I was scared. I moved and boxed super-fast and won on points and went on to win the title and that was the start of our rivalry.

We were both at the England training camps having fierce sparring sessions with each other in preparation for the Commonwealth Games. I was the one who got selected for the Commonwealth Games and it was a bit of a shock to Benny, as he was the favourite to win the ABAs and go to the Commonwealth's so it was understandable there was a bit of bitterness.

We continued training and sparring together on the England training camps and every sparring session was full on with venom in each shot.

Benny got his revenge when he beat me in the 1999 ABAs. I thought I nicked it but many at ringside told me different, that Benny had won it. I was devastated and angry so the rivalry intensified.

Again we trained and sparred together at England training camps and although we respected each other, there was a mutual stand-off.

We both got selected to fight in the 1999 Multi-Nations and both of us got byes in the first round, then we both won our next fights and met in the semi-finals. It was very close but I won the decision and Benny thought he won it. Again the respect was there but so was the rivalry and that was the last time we shared the same ring.

Benny was a great fighter who brought the best out in me. I learned a lot from him and learned a lot about myself in our three fights. He done brilliant as a professional winning the Commonwealth title. He is a family man with great morals in life. We have a good relationship now and huge respect for each other. It was an honour to share the ring with him. I wish him all the best and it is always good to see him now and again for a catch up.

# MICHAEL HALL

## ABA WELTERWEIGHT CHAMPION 1995

I fought Benny in the ABA quarter-finals and didn't really know much about him then but my coach said to me 'make sure you are ready because he'll be fit and strong and in your face all night'. I knew what he meant when I got a look at Benny and saw he had a strong and muscled physique and knew I was in for a tough night. Benny came at me non-stop from start to finish. I was trying to get my jab going to outbox him and keep it at long distance as long as I could, but he closed the range very well. There was no slowing him down and no pushing him back. It was relentless pressure.

When I turned professional I boxed under the name Oscar Hall because there was already someone called Michael Hall. I liked Oscar De La Hoya so that is why I chose the name Oscar.

Years after our amateur fight we did a good bit of sparring together as pros. I didn't know who it was until someone told me as I'm not very good with names. This might sound strange but he has a tattoo on his arm of a bulldog boxer and when I looked at it, it brought it all back, like Déjà vu.

We had some real tear-ups in sparring. The gym was always cold and the ring was on the small side which suited him better than me. You couldn't get no better sparring, it was intense. The closer it got to fight night he seemed to get stronger and sharper. He was first class. When I heard he was bare knuckle boxing I watched some of his fights on the internet. He won the World title and rightly deserved. Congratulations Benny.

# COURTNEY FRY

## 3 X ABA LIGHT-HEAVYWEIGHT CHAMPION 1996, 98 & 01

## COMMONWEALTH GAMES GOLD MEDAL 1998

Kevin Bennett was a true soldier in more ways than one. I remember him drinking until stupid hours in the morning; and then he would be up early sprinting and sparring and doing things the average person would need tons of rest to do. His resilience was second to none and I learnt so much from him in the past. We were England team mates. Kevin Bennett is a true warrior.

# ANDY McLEAN

## 2 X ABA LIGHTWEIGHT CHAMPION 1998 & 00

## 2 X NABC CHAMPION

## COMMONWEALTH GAMES BRONZE MEDAL 1998

I have a funny little story about Kev from the Multi-Nations. We were all tight at the weight and went down for the weigh-in. When Kev got on the scales Steven Bell put his foot on the back of the scales to make them go heavier and when Kev saw his weight the colour drained out of him and he looked devastated. Then when he stepped off everyone was laughing their heads off. He got back on and he was on weight.

Me and Kev were a similar weight but always seemed to miss each other in the ABAs. He was the only one to beat Nigel Wright when Nigel was in his prime. Kev was always someone you didn't want to fight because of his style, he was a pressure fighter. He was all pressure, pressure, pressure. To have a chance with him you had to be 100% fit and at the top of your game.

# JEFF OLLERHEAD

## COMBINED SERVICES CHAMPION

My grandad started the West Wirral amateur boxing club so I started boxing when I was young. I was in the armed forces in the Kings Regiment. I was Kings Champion, then Army champion and Combined Services champion. I was ranked number four in the country behind Joe Calzaghe and Glen Catley.

I became assistant coach for the Army boxing team after being told I couldn't box anymore due to scar tissue on my brain. Not surprising due to the amount of leather and horse hair knuckles that had bounced off my bonce. It would make anyone blow bubbles and window lick for the rest of their days.

I've came across great fighters who could break your jaw and ribs in sparring and Shea Neary was one of them. When I first met Benny I saw greatness in his ring craft and power in both his hands so I called him Banger.

The Army team was brilliant and every man had steal running through their veins. The smell of leather, blood and sweat was addictive to some of us who liked pain and punching flesh.

The first time I saw Benny spar I knew he was one of us, his eyes lit up like a Tiger when he sunk in a body shot and hook to the jaw. He had the style of a mini Mike Tyson and had many hard fights on the circuit. We would fight every week up and down the country or go to foreign shores and spill blood.

We had a great fighting holiday in America when we fought the USA Navy Seals in West Virginia. The yanks must have thought we were punch bags as they put us up in a motel and booked us on various trips like Baseball games. We could drink as much ale as we wanted for free! We were on the piss and getting rat arsed for three days and acquainted many a fair maiden. I recall the yanks laughing and thinking we couldn't tie their shoe laces never mind beat their elite Navy Seals, but we wiped the smiles off their faces when we started knocking out these Adonis looking Seals.

Last fight of the night was Benny against an American/Mexican called Gonzales. They went at it like two pit bulls, what a fight it was. The skill power and speed from both of them was something to see. Benny dug deep and gave Gonzales a fight he'd never forget and won on points. Benny came back to the corner with a cheeky grin on his face and Gonzales was on the USA Olympic team.

Benny is so modest and humble, he is a gentleman. He never bad mouthed anybody and always let his fists do the talking in the ring.

# **KIRKY**

### FORMER PRO FIGHTER

I remember lying in our scratchers one day in the Army and imagining what the future would hold and what we wanted to achieve. Benny dreamed of becoming a professional champion and that dream later became a reality through a lot of hard work and sacrifice. I turned pro in Belfast but never reached the heights Benny did. I wanted to be a paid fighter and he wanted to be a champion.

Once when I was fighting for the Army in Portsmouth and I was having a right old ding dong of a battle, when I heard a Brummie voice shout 'Come on Adrian' and I landed a big shot and knocked my opponent out. I have that video and will always be thankful to Benny for shouting what he did, when he did.

When the boxing team coach came in the gym with his clipboard of names of the days sparring and who would be sparring with whom, and even though I loved a good tear up, I always dreaded getting drawn against Benny. I would always have sore ribs because body shots were Benny the lung buster's favourite punch. Even when Benny was an amateur he had a pro style. I watched him have some brilliant sparring sessions that you'd pay good money to watch.

Benny called me 'Kirky the Sponge' and it soon stuck as all the Army lads started to call me it. It is because I never slipped any punches. Whenever I meet up with the boxing lads of yesteryear I always get called that thanks to Benny.

Since he retired from the pro game and achieving his dream of becoming a pro champion, he couldn't shake the bug and started bare knuckle boxing and became World Champion.

He is a gentleman who has time for everyone and is always there to help anyone. In a nutshell he is an absolute diamond and they broke the mould after he was born.

# BILLY BESSEY

## ABA SUPER-HEAVYWEIGHT CHAMPION 1999

I had a bit of trouble in a night club once and the guy was pals with all the bouncers so I was told to leave. There where Doormen lined up all the way down the stairs and I turned to Benny (it was me who was getting thrown out but Benny still came out with me and had my back) and said:

"You know we are getting done here don't you?"

Benny just laughed and said:

"I know. It's good isn't it",

When we got outside nothing happened. If you want anyone back to back with you it's Benny.

I have never been hit as hard in sparring as I was against Benny. Every time he hit me I remember thinking 'I'm going here, I'm going'. I was 17 stone at the time and he was about 10 stone. I couldn't believe the power he had. I don't know how lightweights and light-welters could stand up to that. I was a heavyweight and out on my feet. It was a different kind of power. Pound for pound power. He was something else.

# MARK VICKERS

## WOLVERHAMPTON ABC BOXER AND COACH

Benny was a man who dedicated his life to perfecting the sweet science. He was a man who became a champion boxer as an amateur and a professional. He was a man who took the bare knuckle world by storm to become world champion. He destroyed many a fighter's soul and they were never the same fighter's again. He is humble, a gentleman and very genuine and is a man I can call my friend.

Kevin Bennett I salute you.

# BRAD HARRIS

## BARE KNUCKLE BOXER

I fought Kev twice. The first time he made my boxing go out the window. He wouldn't let me have any distance to get into a rhythm and the body shots he hit me with were nothing like I'd ever felt before.

I done my homework for the second fight and thought I had it in me to beat him but he was so strong and just kept coming forward with steel intensity. I gave it my best shot but he was just unstoppable and those body punches I can still feel to this day.

I'll say something else about him he's one of the most respectful men I've ever met.

# ALAN TEMPLE

### ABA FEATHERWEIGHT CHAMPION 1992

### ABA LIGHT-WELTERWEIGHT CHAMPION 1994

### BRITISH MASTERS LIGHTWEIGHT CHAMPION

I sparred with Kev a couple of times when Neil Fannan and Dave Garside brought him to our gym. Kev was a banger so I just kept on the outside and countered his strong attacks. I would have been a fool to stand and trade with him. He had heavy hands and knocked out some good pros. I was down to fight Kev twice but unfortunately it never came off. I think it would have been a good fight. Kevin is a sound lad and a very good fighter who had a great career and I have lots of respect for him.

# BOBBY VANZIE

## BRITISH LIGHTWEIGHT CHAMPION

## COMMONWEALTH LIGHTWEIGHT CHAMPION

Kevin became Commonwealth champ after I retired. He was a strong and well-schooled box-fighter. I actually saw one of his bare knuckle fights. What a tough man.

# SEAN GEORGE

## BARE KNUCKLE BOXER

I remember my nose going splat and crack a few times with that overhand right in my fight against Kev. He hit me with a terrific jab in the second round and he couldn't have hit me any harder, I just survived the rest of the round and my eye closed in the third.

My corner wanted to pull me out but I have the heart of a lion and wouldn't hear of it and it went the full five rounds bare knuckle title fight distance. It was voted BKB fight of the year and everyone has said that it's the best BKB fight ever held in a ring and I still get people pulling me up and talking about it. The 500 people who were present knew they had just witnessed something special. What an honour it was to share the ring with such a fine champion.

Kevin Bennett is a true gentleman and will always be the champion in my eyes I have so much respect for him. I always talk about him he is an inspiration to us all, a true champion.

# ANDREW BUCHANAN

## GOLD MEDAL MULTI-NATIONS 1999

## NABC CHAMPION

I remember Kevin from the England squad and also the boxing circuit of the late 90s. We boxed on the same team out in Denmark and also in the Multi-Nations when they were held in Liverpool.

The squad went out on the town after it was over, I was sharing a room with Kev, but I had to get a random drug test after I won the Gold Medal so I met up with them later. I can't remember much about the night as I was trying to keep up with Kevin, pint for pint, and with him being a squaddie he could certainly sink a few.

It was about five am and all the squad were still drinking in the only place that was open which happened to be a gay club! It was a surreal experience to say the least.

I had to be up early to catch a train home but Kev made sure I was ok and didn't miss my train. He was always a character at the boxing shows and I had some great laughs with him back then. I wish him all the best and thanks for the memories.

# TED FOST

## STAFF SERGEANT AND ARMY BOXING COACH

I trained the Army boxing team in Germany. It was seriously talented with former Olympians and national champions. Kev tried out for us and I was impressed, he was only 17 or 18 and the youngest on the squad.

I lived with my wife and children in a house about five miles outside camp and offered Kev a room to keep him from being led astray by the squaddies and he jumped at the chance.

When we fought in the finals in Germany he jumped straight into a title fight. He was really cocky and telling everyone he was going to knock his opponent out in the first round. I'm not being funny but the team we were up against were all very hard men and shit hot fighters.

Kev went hell for leather in the first round and tried a bit too hard for the early finish. The first round ends and I'm sat on the stool on the floor outside the ring and he shouts "Oi what are you doing?" and I shout back "I didn't bring any water or a towel because you said you were going to knock him out in the first round so I didn't bother".

The fight went the distance and it was a belter and Kev got the nod without any water.

He stayed with my squad for a few years and I entered him in any championships he wanted. He wanted to fight and we went on the road and travelled around Europe taking on anybody.

There was this one guy I remember who had a very big reputation and was as hard as nails, never spoke just growled, had a nasty stare and a chiselled physique. At the weigh in Kev thought he'd get into the blokes head and shouted out loud to all the officials:

"Before I fight him he needs to have a wash because he smells".

It was pure gold from Bennett but that set the tone for the night and my god, what a slam bang affair it was. Every punch was thrown with bad intentions from both sides and it went the distance. It was a close one and Kev won it.

Kev never lost a fight for me and we went around Europe, Northern Ireland, Republic of Ireland, Germany, Scotland, Wales, and all over England.

I was in the Army for 27 years and knew thousands of people. I've got 13 medals and fought in every campaign. I've had guys by the side of me with holes in them. If there's anyone I'd want to stand back to back with it is Kev, and I have done on a few occasions but those stories are for private conversation. He is one of the best men I have ever met in my life.

# DARREN DAZZO WILLIAMS

## BRITISH FEATHERWEIGHT CHAMPION

We had just come back from a morning run at the Army barracks in Aldershot and were having a shower. I was scratching like mad and so was Benny and he said 'what are you scratching for?' and I said 'probably the same reason you are'.

The first thing that came into my mind was that we must have been with the same woman but it proved not to be the case as it wasn't a STD. He showed me his hands with all the scabs on the inside of his fingers and I had the same. We went to the garrison hospital and I pushed Benny's name forward in front of mine to see the nurse and he gave me a mucky look. We were both diagnosed with scabies and got a prescription for calamine lotion. We had to stay out of the gym for a week while it cleared up.

The nurse told us it can be contacted through sweat glands and we found out that one of the boxers on the Army team had scabies and we caught it by wearing sweaty boxing gloves. All the boxing gloves and other bits and bobs were thrown away and new ones ordered. I laugh when I think about it.

We both fought New York champions. We had to pretend we boxed for Kingston or something because we were both Army. I won my fight and as soon as I got out the ring there was a can of lager waiting for me. It's a squaddie thing. It was the same for Benny when he won.

When I used to spar with him he was a nightmare to hit and he hurt me with body shots because he could bang.

I think the best fight I saw Benny in was against Roy Rutherford who was ABA champion, what a fight it was. I thought Benny won but they gave Rutherford the decision. He came up to Benny after the fight and said 'you won that'. It was nice of him to say that.

I had the privilege of watching him as an amateur and a professional and in my opinion he had everything.

# IAN COOPER

### ABA MIDDLEWEIGHT CHAMPION 1997

### NORTHERN AREA SUPER-MIDDLEWEIGHT CHAMPION

I was there the night Kevin broke Michael Hunter's nose in sparring. Kev was pulling his punches as well so you can imagine the power he had. Michael was in a mood for weeks over it.

We sparred a lot together when we first turned pro. I was over a stone heavier than him and he hurt me a lot, every spar was competitive. I didn't think anybody his weight could beat him.

He would constantly be in your face coming forward bobbing and weaving and coming in with hooks and uppercuts, bang, bang, bang. He would make you fight every second of every round and I would be over the moon when the bell rang for a bit of rest bite.

I would hit him with everything I had and put power in my shots and sometimes he'd nod to acknowledge it, but he used to just take it and never take a backward step, he was so tough. I always tried to put him on the back foot but I could never do it no matter how hard I tried.

I sparred all over the place with top quality men in places like Liverpool and Manchester, Gary Locket included, but none of them were a patch on Kevin Bennett.

He did everything properly, never cut corners, run every morning, trained like a demon. I think the discipline was instilled in him in his Army days. Kevin is a lovely lad and deserves all the credit he gets.

# PETER JACKSON

## MIDLANDS AREA SUPER-MIDDLEWEIGHT CHAMPION

When I was at Warley ABC there was an article on the cork clip board about a lad called Kevin Bennett who was tipped to follow in the footsteps of Pat Cowdell, our local hero.

One day Benny turned up at our gym and the coach announced to everyone that Kevin Bennett the England International is here to do some sparring with a few of you. Benny just smiled at everyone and nodded.

I was hungry and wanted to impress so when I got in the ring with him I was throwing shots boom, boom.

He was slipping them and I couldn't land a punch and I was thinking 'what the hell is going on here' but Benny was showing me the art of boxing, hit and not get hit. Then he slipped to the left and hit me with a body shot and it took every bit of air out of my body and I literally couldn't breathe. He just looked at me and nodded his head. He taught me so much that day.

Another time he came to the gym and when he started shadow boxing, the coach told us all to watch him. The way he moved and his footwork was amazing. He was a role model to us all.

I'll tell you about one night years later when we had been out for a drink. It had been a quiet night and we were about to get in a taxi when these two guys shout 'that's our cab' and the biggest one put his arm across the door so no one could get in. Then he turned to my brother- who wouldn't say boo to a goose- and punched him in the face!

In a split second the big guy had been dropped and his mate ran away and left him. Benny chased after him and caught him and put him down with a sweet shot. He then said to the guy:

"The reason why I came after you was because you ran off and left your mate".

This was a long time ago but I still remember thinking 'wow'. His principles were so strong. He was a role model for me and for me to be near him and watch him, learn from him and be hit by him, I considered it an honour. He bleached his hair blond once so I bleached mine blond that's how much I admired him.

I would drive for three hours up to Hartlepool to spar with him and Ian Cooper. It was great being around them and meeting a lot of good people, priceless memories.

# NEIL FANNAN

## FORMER LIGHT-MIDDLEWEIGHT CONTENDER

### PROFESSIONAL BOXING COACH

Benny is one of the most talented lads I've trained and I enjoyed our little Journey. We went to Ireland, Wales, Scotland, all over the British Isles. It was me who gave him the nickname the Bulldog.

Sometimes he didn't like to be in the limelight and in front of the cameras and would rather fight without them. When he won the Commonwealth title and was swallowing a lot of blood because of a broken nose, I said to him 'suck it up Benny and do it for your kids, make them proud' and as you know he won the title but had to go to hospital after. When I walked in the hospital he said "Neil when you told me to do it for my kids, do it for myself, do it …I done it for you. Take the belt it's yours." I wouldn't take the belt because it was his, but I never forgot what he said, it stuck in my mind. As a trainer it's nice to be appreciated and it was a nice thing for him to say.

Sometimes you need a bit of luck and circumstances to be right. The Graham Earl fight for one. That fight should have been stopped in the fifth round. Under any other circumstances it would have been stopped.

After we had done all the training and hard work, Earl pulled out at the last minute and that done our plug in. The fight got put back but we had to stay in training camp for another four weeks and Benny trained for about ten weeks for it altogether.

# MALLY RICHARDSON

### BARE KNUCKLE BOXER

I remember standing in the ring, face to face with him and thinking, 'I've got this in the bag' but looks can be deceiving, as we know. The bell sounded and I went straight for him throwing big punches and caught him with some good shots. He didn't even flinch and walked through them like they were nothing!

Then he went to work on my body and I've never felt body punches like them, I thought I was going to shit myself! Hence to say the fight ended in the first round after I had been down three times.

Whenever I see Kev at shows we always have a chat, he is a great chap and a proper gent.

# GEORGE TELFER

## SCOTTISH ABA CHAMPION

## SCOTLAND INTERNATIONAL

I was Scottish champion and had won 26 fights in a row when I fought Kevin Bennett. I beat Barry Morrison twice and he went on to become British champion. I didn't know anything about Kevin when we fought but we went toe-to-toe and it was a hard fight. We both had come forward styles which made it a great scrap. It was a close call and he got the nod. He was a top fighter and he brought my winning streak to an end.

# DEAN PHILLIPS

## COMMONWEALTH LIGHTWEIGHT TITLE CHALLENGER

I took a little time out and watched Kevin Bennett fight and knew I would face him when I went back to the game and I did go back.

I had the appropriate number of fights, all wins, which prepared me well and I got the call to fight Kevin Bennett for the Commonwealth Lightweight title.

Everything was going great in training and I was getting some excellent sparring in preparation and felt I was right at the top of my game.

Around ten days before the fight I suffered a ruptured pectoral underneath the armpit in sparring so I never sparred the week leading up to it. I was still doing sprint intervals and long distance running. I considered pulling out as it affected my left arm which is my best weapon. However, I decided to crack on with it due to the opportunity to improve my status and let my arm heal itself for the last ten days.

I was a good pressure fighter and Kevin fought the right fight regardless of the situation and prevented me from opening up and pressurising.

Afterwards I shook his hand and told him he fought the right fight. I think Kevin knew I was a dangerous fighter because I seem to remember him telling my corner men.

I have turned my back on the sport due to the politics involved. Promoters run the show and some are not nice people and just use the fighters. We are just a number to them to fill in the gaps and I would not encourage my child to fight professionally.

Training is great for them and the amateur game does wonders for young people but the moment money is involved, it's a different story altogether.

I have spoken to Kevin since our title fight and wish him all the best.

# GLENN McCLARNON

BRITISH WELTERWEIGHT TITLE CHALLENGER

Kev tried to put me on the back foot but I was just too big for him to make me budge. He kept coming forward making the fight. He was a good boxer, tricky and fast with good feet.

# DAZ DUGAN

## COMBINED SERVICES FEATHERWEIGHT CHAMPION

We were on the piss quite a lot in the Army days but that's what squaddies like to do. We had a five minute rule when tapping a woman up. If you weren't sorted in five minutes, the other would come over and get in between and say things like "Are you really wanting to shag that" as well as other things which usually meant either of us getting slapped round the face. We thought it was funny at the time but you wouldn't get away with stuff like that now.

We had some crazy nights that can only be spoken of in private conversations but that was all part of the squaddie life. A couple of times while we were out drinking I walked up behind Kev and got my old boy old and pissed in his pocket. Very funny you must admit.

Kev was a great fighter. He was a crowd pleaser and loved a tear up.

# JOHN SPENCER

## BARE KNUCKLE BOXER

Kevin had the most brutal body shots I've ever felt in 300 fights. They were crippling. They took my breath away and my lungs were on fire and I couldn't breathe. Absolutely brutal shots I'll never forget.

# LUKE COPE

## JUNIOR ABA CHAMPION

## ENGLISH BELT HOLDER

Kevin was 41 years old and having his last ever fight when I got the call to spar with him. We sparred for six rounds, once a week for six weeks, and each week I could see and feel the difference in his power and sharpness. He had some brilliant little tricks inside the ring and I learned from him. Kevin is a genuine man who likes to see others do well and always has time to say hello to people. He's a top bloke in and out of the ring.

Young Amateur

Army Gym waiting to Spar

Working hard in the Gym

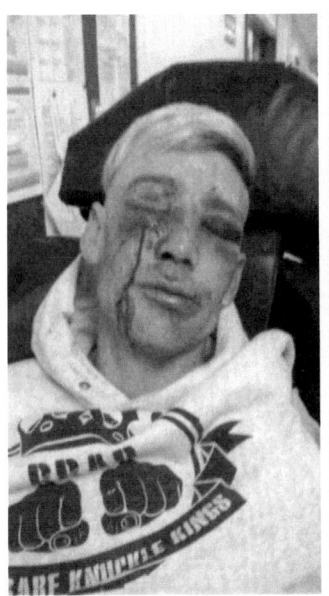

LEFT: Sean George after our fight. He received a broken nose, fractured cheekbone and concussion. RIGHT: My Proud Parents when I won the BKB World Title

First defence of the Title

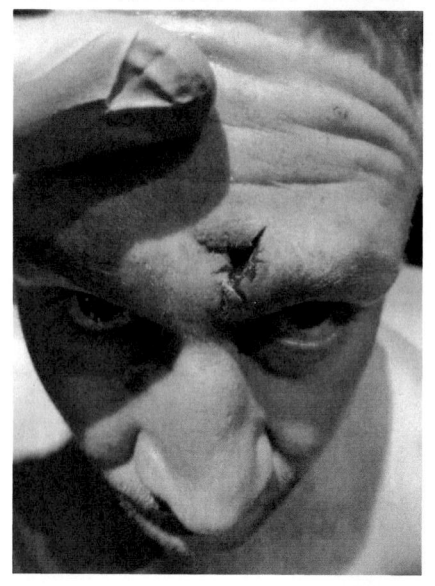

Hole in the Head

Day after winning second World Title.

I retired less than a week later.

Wedding Day

All six of us: Jake, Keeley, Molly, Zack, Gemma and myself

## ALSO AVAILABLE FROM WARCRY PRESS

NORTHERN WARRIOR
by Richy Horsley

BATTLING BOWES
by Richy Horsley

UNFINISHED AGONY
by Jamie Boyle

FURTHER AGONY: ONE MORE ROUND WITH SYKES
by Jamie Boyle

TALES OF PUGILISM
by Jamie Boyle

SWEET AGONY
by Paul Sykes

THE FORGOTTEN CHAMP
John L.Gardner with Nick Towle

BLOOD IS ONLY READ SWEAT
Dave Radford with Nick Towle

DODGER: PUPIL OF THE KRAYS
by Steve Tully

A STIFF SENTENCE
by John Keenan